**A2**

# Olive Green
# English

The authors of film dialogues and vocabulary lists: Wojciech Wojtasiak, Magdalena Warżała-Wojtasiak

The authors of grammar: Marta Borowiak-Dostatnia (A1-B1), Marcin Mortka (B2-C1)

The authors of interactive dialogues and vocabulary lists: Marta Borowiak-Dostatnia, Monika Glińska

Proofreading: Monika Glińska, Alicja Jankowiak, Natalia Wajda

Edited by: Alicja Jankowiak

Recordings: Graham Crawford, Joanna Haracz-Lewandowska, Jagoda Lembicz, Dale Taylor, Marianna Waters-Sobkowiak

Cover design: Marcin Stanisławski

Graphic design and composition: Wioletta Kowalska / Violet Design

Stock photos: © Fotolia.com

# Olive Green English A2

**Publisher** Chung Kyudo

**Editors** Cho Sangik, Hong Inpyo, Kim Taeyeon, Kwak Bitna

**Designers** Kim Nakyung, Yoon Hyunjoo, Im Miyoung

First Published December 2017
By Darakwon Bldg., 211, Munbal-ro, Paju-si, Gyeonggi-do 10881, Republic of Korea
Tel. 82-2-736-2031 (Ext. 550-553)

© Copyright SuperMemo World sp. z o.o., 2017
   SuperMemo is the registered trademark by SuperMemo World sp. z o.o.

© Copyright for the South Korean edition by Darakwon, 2017

All rights reserved. No part of this publication may be reproduced, stored in a retrieval system, or transmitted in any form or by any means, electronic, mechanical, photocopying, or otherwise, without the prior consent of the copyright owner. Refund after purchase is possible only according to the company regulations. Contact the above telephone number for any inquiries.
Consumer damages caused by loss, damage, etc. can be compensated according to the consumer dispute resolution standards announced by the Korea Fair Trade Commission.
An incorrectly collated book will be exchanged.

Price ₩12,000
ISBN: 978-89-277-0952-7 14740
      978-89-277-0950-3 14740 (set)

http://www.darakwon.co.kr
Main Book / Free MP3 Available Online
7 6 5 4 3 2 1   17 18 19 20 21

# Table of contents

**Introduction** .................................................................................................. **4**

Scene 1 (13): In the middle of nowhere ....................................................... **8**
Expressing opinions • Expressing preferences • Suggestions / Social conversations • TV shows and celebrities • Arguing your opinion • Keeping the conversation going • Finishing the conversation

Scene 2 (14): Gentle art of blackmail ......................................................... **16**
to be going to • will • Present Continuous • Possessive pronouns
Planning your holidays • At the travel agency • Booking a holiday • Describing your dream holiday

Scene 3 (15): Home, sweet home ............................................................... **26**
Present Simple (schedules) • will (predictions) / Giving directions • Describing a town • Household chores and their division • Agreeing and disagreeing • Finding a compromise

Scene 4 (16): Negotiations .......................................................................... **34**
may • could • shall • would like to / TV game shows • Participating in a competition • Negotiating and expressing opposition • Looking for ways to resolve a conflict • Weights and measures • Means of transport

Scene 5 (17): Visiting Cloutier .................................................................... **44**
(not) have to • must(n't) • everybody • somebody • nobody • anybody / Buying gifts and works of art • Discussing art • Describing objects (appearance, size, colour, shape, material etc.) • Expressing delight

Scene 6 (18): At Alfie's place ..................................................................... **54**
Present Perfect vs. Past Simple • Past Simple (would, could)
Radio interview • Talking about your background, education, jobs, past choices etc.

Scene 7 (19): David in a trap ..................................................................... **62**
Present Continuous (describing states) • Countable and uncountable nouns • a lot of
Shopping list • Replenishing your groceries • Take-away • Cuisine of different countries • Expressing surprise • Preparing food and describing the steps

Scene 8 (20): Confrontation ....................................................................... **70**
Past Continuous • Past Continuous vs. Past Simple / Sharing stories with friends • Expressing interest

Scene 9 (21): Grave digging ....................................................................... **80**
Passive voice
Expressing your opinion in a street survey • Environmental protection • Environment pollution • Renewable energy sources

Scene 10 (22): Another confrontation....................................................... **88**
Superlative of adjectives • Adverbs • Comparative and superlative of adverbs / Working as a journalist • Dangerous occupations – firefighter, stuntman etc. • Safety and harm at work • Gender stereotypes in professions

Scene 11 (23): Great, now we're trapped................................................... **96**
Question tags • Interrogative pronouns
At the shops – buying products, asking for help, specifying the amount and weight • Naming and describing foodstuffs

Scene 12 (24): It's up to you, David........................................................... **106**
Zero conditional • Time clauses • Complex sentences
Helping with hardware • Giving instructions and advice to a beginner • Describing computers and electronic equipment

**Translation** ............................................................................................. **114**

# Introduction

**Olive Green** is an innovative course for those who want to learn English from the beginning in a way that is both modern and efficient. It is the perfect combination of fun and effective learning of the highest order.

The **Olive Green** multimedia course is based on an **interactive action film**, where you can decide what course the plot will take, as well as play some arcade-type and language games. The course is divided into 12 film scenes for each language skill level.

## What is the best way to learn with the **Olive Green** course?

To begin with, watch the right **film scene** in the multimedia course. We encourage you to watch it several times, so that you can gradually get used to the natural pronunciation you hear and make decisions during interactions. The **subtitles** (available in English and many other languages) will help you understand the content of the dialogue. If you are learning English from scratch, first watch each scene with subtitles in your own language (if available), then with English subtitles, and finally without subtitles. Next, read the **text of the film dialogue** in the book. Then listen to the MP3 recordings of the dialogue, and lastly try to read the text aloud.

Each scene in the book is accompanied by a **list of new words and expressions**. Read them and find them in the dialogue to see how they are used in context, and then listen to the recording of the list.

In the next step, please read the **grammar explanations** describing the most important topics introduced in each film dialogue. You will find many examples of typical applications of all the new structures in these sections.

The multimedia course also includes **interactive dialogues** to let you practice in a variety of communication situations and develop the skills necessary for a conversation in English. Additionally, selected variants of these dialogues have been included in the book, together with the lists of new words and phrases that will help you expand your vocabulary for each topic.

Last but not least, read the **cultural commentary** that will introduce you to some interesting aspects of the culture of the English-speaking countries. The language of the commentaries is simple, but if you are just starting your adventure with English, it may be hard to understand. In that case, please remember that it is always better to try to analyze and understand the general meaning of any English text on your own first – especially if you have been working with the course for some time. Consulting a dictionary for definitions or equivalents of the words that may be new to you should generally be your "second best" option.

To those who wish to continue learning English with **Olive Green**, we recommend the rest part of the course at the other levels.

Enjoy your learning!
The SuperMemo World team
& Darakwon Olive Green team

# Olive Green

## level A2

# Scene 1 (13)  Film dialogue and vocabulary

**Read the dialogue between Alfie (A) and Cloutier (C). Check the list of words and phrases below.**

How is he doing, Cloutier?

C: Fine, fine! Marco's a strong, tough, young man. I'm sure he'll wake up very soon.

A: Yeah, maybe … I still think you should cover him. Hypothermia is a nasty thing, you know. She's such a thoughtful girl! Even now, when I want to … kill Olive with my bare hands, I have to bloody admit it! Deep inside she's a nice and kind person!

C: Kind? I disagree! Look at that poor boy!

A: Nah! It's just business. She didn't kill us, did she? She gave us the blankets, food … even a bucket! We'll be all right … Spend a few days in the shed, then she'll let us out! It's practically a holiday!

C: You are insane, Alfie! Insane! Why don't you keep your mouth shut?

A: I can't! I love talking and socialising with people! You are a Frenchman – aren't Frenchmen sociable and talkative?

C: I hate to say it but I don't feel very sociable right now. Maybe it's because I'm locked in here, in the middle of nowhere, with a dying man and a crazy Brit.

A: He's not dying! … How about a snack? We really should eat something! I believe it's breakfast time! We've got some … well, three candy bars and some … ham sandwiches and some cheese sandwiches.

C: I'd like a ham sandwich, please. I generally like to start my day with some meat in my stomach!

A: Say … this tastes kind of funny. Can you … pass the bucket, please?

# level A2

## Vocabulary

| | | | |
|---|---|---|---|
| do | 해나가다, (일이) 되어가다 | socialize | (사람들과) 사귀다, 어울리다 |
| strong | 강한 | Frenchman | 프랑스인 |
| tough | 튼튼한 | sociable | 사교적인 |
| wake up | 깨다, 일어나다 | hate to do | ~하고 싶지 않다 |
| soon | 금방, 곧 | feel | (기분이) 들다 |
| cover | 덮다 | locked | 갇힌 |
| hypothermia | 저체온증 | in the middle of nowhere | 외딴곳에 |
| nasty | 고약한 | dying | 죽어가는 |
| thoughtful | 자상한 | crazy | 미친 |
| kill with bare hands | 맨손으로 죽이다 | Brit | 영국인 |
| bloody | 굉장히, 지독히, 몹시 | snack | 간식 |
| admit | 인정하다 | eat | 먹다 |
| deep inside | 마음속 깊은 곳에서 | breakfast | 아침 식사 |
| person | 사람 | candy bar | 초코바 |
| disagree | 동의하지 않다 | ham | 햄 |
| blanket | 담요 | sandwich | 샌드위치 |
| food | 음식 | cheese | 치즈 |
| bucket | 양동이 | generally | 보통, 대개 |
| spend | (시간을) 보내다 | start | 시작하다 |
| practically | 사실상, 거의 | meat | 고기 |
| holiday | 휴가 | stomach | 위장, 배 |
| insane | 제정신이 아닌, 미친 | taste | ~한 맛이 나다 |
| keep one's mouth shut | 입을 다물고 있다 | pass | 건네주다 |

# Grammar explanations

## 의견 표현하기: *love, like, hate, prefer*

### love

Robert **loves** spend**ing** time in his gallery. = Robert **loves to** spend time in his gallery.
Robert는 그의 화랑에서 시간 보내는 것을 좋아합니다.

Beatrice **loves** work**ing** in her garden. = Beatrice **loves to** work in her garden.
Beatrice는 그녀의 정원에서 일하는 것을 좋아합니다.

### like

Cloutier **likes** hav**ing** a ham sandwich in the mornings. = Cloutier **likes to** have a ham sandwich in the mornings.   Cloutier는 아침마다 햄 샌드위치를 먹는 것을 좋아합니다.

You really **like** danc**ing**, don't you? = You really **like to** dance, don't you?
당신은 춤 추는 것을 정말 좋아하는군요, 그렇지 않나요?

### prefer

I don't like tea. I **prefer** drink**ing** coffee. = I **prefer to** drink coffee.
저는 차를 좋아하지 않아요. 커피 마시는 것을 더 좋아하죠.

Olive **prefers** liv**ing** in big cities like New York. = Olive **prefers to** live in big cities like New York.   Olive는 뉴욕과 같은 대도시에 사는 것을 선호합니다.

### hate

I **hate** tell**ing** lies. = I **hate to** tell lies.   저는 거짓말하는 것을 싫어해요.

We **hate** mov**ing** house every 2 years. = We **hate to** move house every 2 years.
우리는 2년마다 이사하는 것을 싫어해요.


## 좋아하는 것 표현하기 Expressing preferences

-**ing** ➜ 어떤 것이 우리에게 즐거움을 주고, 그것이 우리가 좋아하는 일일 때

**to** ➜ 어떤 것이 우리의 습관이나 선호일 때, 또는 우리에게 알맞거나 유용하거나 현명한 선택일 때

### -ing

I **like** socialis**ing** with people.
나는 사람들과 어울리는 것을 좋아합니다. (새 친구를 사귀고 함께 시간 보내는 것을 좋아함)

Olive **prefers** jogg**ing** to watching TV.
Olive는 TV를 보는 것보다 조깅을 하는 것을 선호합니다. (조깅을 좋아하고 조깅을 하면 즐겁지만, TV를 보는 것은 좋아하지 않음)

We **love** travell**ing** with our friends.
우리는 친구들과 함께 여행하는 것을 좋아합니다. (그게 바로 '우리'가 좋아하는 여행 방식임)

Vlad **hates** be**ing** photographed.
Vlad는 사진 찍히는 것을 싫어합니다. (어렸을 때부터 사진 찍히는 것이라면 질색임)

**to**

Robert **likes to** socialize with people at his parties.
Robert는 파티에서 사람들과 어울리는 것을 좋아합니다. (실제로 좋아하지는 않지만 사업상 중요함)

People **hate to** give bad news.   사람들은 나쁜 소식을 전하는 것을 싫어합니다.
(사람들은 다른 사람에게 나쁜 소식을 전할 때 슬프고 속상해함)

Olive **loves to** go to local museums in the places she visits.
Olive는 자신이 방문하는 지역의 미술관에 가는 것을 좋아합니다.
(다른 지역에 방문할 경우에 그런 것이지, 원래 미술관에 가는 것을 좋아한다는 뜻은 아님)

I **prefer to** have white wine with stew. It tastes better.
저는 스튜에 화이트 와인을 곁들이는 것을 선호합니다. 그러면 맛이 더 좋습니다. (스튜를 먹을 때면, 화이트 와인을 마심)


### 제안하기: *how about, why don't, should*

➔ **how about** + 명사/-ing

   **How about** a snack?   간식 먹을래요?

   **How about** play**ing** chess?   체스 할까요?


➔ **why don't** + I/you/he/she/it/we/they + 동사원형

   **Why don't you give** me a ham sandwich?   햄 샌드위치를 주시겠어요?

   **Why don't we think** how to get out of here?   여기서 빠져나갈 방법을 생각해 보는 게 어때?


➔ I/you/he/she/it/we/they + **should** + 동사원형

   **We should cover** him. He is dying.   우리는 그를 덮어줘야 해요. 그가 죽어가고 있어요.

   **We should eat** something! We haven't eaten since yesterday.
   우리는 뭐라도 먹어야 해요! 어제부터 아무것도 못 먹었잖아요.

level A2  Scene 1 (13)

# Communication situations

**Read the following dialogues between a couple of friends talking about television shows.**

What about a talent show, you know, dancing, singing, performing ... I watch them from time to time.

### Dialogue 1

**Man:** Me too. I'm a big fan of any music talent show.

**Woman:** Oh, are you?

**Man:** I am. I think they are a good way to success.

**Woman:** That's true but still ... I think people in those shows are dishonest and desperate for success.

**Man:** That's not entirely true. You are judging them too harshly.

**Woman:** Am I? As far as I'm concerned, people who enter such contests are naïve.

**Man:** I don't agree at all. I'd say they are determined.

**Woman:** Meaning?

**Man:** Well, some people live for success.

**Woman:** I know. I have nothing against that but still - it's not the best way for me.

**Man:** So what's the best way in your opinion?

**Woman:** Luck and talent are crucial here.

**Man:** You may have a point here but on the other hand, it's not enough just to have talent.

**Woman:** Oh, I'm sure it's not enough. A bit of luck would do as well.

**Man:** Well, no doubt about it.

**Woman:** So we agree at least in part. That's a good start of the evening.

---

**talent** 장기, 소질 | **show** 쇼 | **perform** 연기하다, 공연하다 | **be desperate for** ~에 기를 쓰다, ~을 간절히 원하다 | **harshly** 엄하게 | **as far as I'm concerned** 내 생각에는, 나로서는 | **enter a contest** 대회에 참가하다 | **at all** 전혀 | **determined** 결연한, 굳게 결심한

## Dialogue 2

**Man:** I see what you mean but I don't like such shows.

**Woman:** You don't? Why is that?

**Man:** I find them irritating.

**Woman:** What exactly do you find irritating?

**Man:** Well, I can't stand these glossy, smug and perfectly dressed celebrities.

**Woman:** You mean the jury?

**Man:** That's right. They are cruel and heartless.

**Woman:** That's true but that's the showbiz for you: ruthless.

**Man:** That's a good point. But it's sad, isn't it?

**Woman:** Indeed. It is sad. So let's move on to something more pleasant. Would you like a snack?

---

**glossy** 겉만 번지르르한; 윤기가 흐르는 | **cruel** 잔인한, 무정한 | **ruthless** 무자비한, 인정사정없는 | **move on** (새로운 주제로) 넘어가다

## Dialogue 3

**Man:** I see. Personally, I'm not sure if I like them.

**Woman:** Me too. Sometimes I find it all quite pathetic.

**Man:** Let me guess. You don't like the teasing jury, do you?

**Woman:** I don't think I follow you.

**Man:** Well, in my opinion they are very unfair. And they are just celebrities, not experts!

**Woman:** Yes, that's true, but that's the idea of the show.

---

**personally** 개인적으로 | **tease** (짓궂게) 괴롭히다, 놀리다, 골리다 | **I don't think I follow you.** 무슨 말인지 모르겠는걸.

# Vocabulary plus

**age discrimination** 연령 차별

**as far as I know** 내가 알기로는

**at this point** 현 시점에서는

**bad-tempered** 곧잘 성질을 내는

**be most likely to** ~할 가능성이 가장 크다

**bill** (국회에 제출된) 법안

**competitor** 경쟁자

**crass** 무신경한, 어리석은

**drop the subject** 이야기를 그만두다

**equally well** 똑같이 잘

**essential** 가장 중요한, 필수적인

**feel about** ~에 대해 (~하게) 생각하다

**feel strongly about** ~에 대해 확고한 견해를 가지다

**find common ground** 합의점을 찾다

**get at** ~를 계속 나무라다

**good-looking** 잘생긴

**hard-working** 열심히 일하는, 근면한

**humble** 겸손한

**I take your point.** 무슨 말인지 알겠어.

**if you ask me** 내 개인적인 생각으로는

**leave it at that** 그 정도로 해 두다

**make money** 돈을 벌다

**mock** 놀리다, 조롱하다

**not my cup of tea** 내 관심사가 아닌

**once-in-a-lifetime** 일생에 한 번뿐인

**ordinary** 평범한, 보통의

**poll** 투표

**positive feedback** 긍정적인 피드백

**Prime Minister** 총리, 수상

**propose** 제안하다, 제의하다

**remind** (기억하도록) 다시 한번 말해 주다

**ridiculous** 말도 안 되는, 터무니없는

**say hello to** ~에게 인사하다

**self-confident** 자기를 과신하는; 자신 있는

**sense of humour** 유머 감각

**staged** 연출된, 일부러 꾸민

**That's the idea.** 바로 그거야.

**The grass is always greener on the other side of the fence.** 남의 떡이 더 커 보이는 법이지. (울타리 저 편 잔디가 더 푸르다.)

**to my mind** 내 생각에는

**up to a point** 어느 정도는

**what it's going to be like** 어떨지

**You've lost me.** 무슨 말인지 모르겠어.

# Cultural tips

## Did you know that …?

In the UK, snacks are quite popular between meals; the British people love snacks! Crisps and chocolate are among the favourites. Crisps come in a variety of flavours, such as cheese and onion, bacon, salt and vinegar, to name just a few. The list of top snacks also includes: jelly babies, biscuits, chocolate bars, and malt balls.

# Scene 2 (14)  Film dialogue and vocabulary

Read the dialogue between Murray (M) and David (D). Check the list of words and phrases below.

So, David, this situation with Olive … It's very serious! What are we gonna do about it?

I don't know that, but I do remember you tried to kill me last night!

**M:** Did I? You got that wrong! You see, I've done some research on Miss Green. She's a professional art thief. Cold and calculating woman …

**D:** Last night … Did she steal one of your paintings?

**M:** No, she did something far worse. She stole some confidential business data. So I need you to find her and get it back!

**D:** No way! No way! In fact, after this conversation, I'm calling my sergeant at the station telling him everything about you …

**M:** You're certainly not! Olive's helping my enemies destroy me and my business! And you helped her! What's your sergeant gonna do with you? You made a mistake, but you're a good policeman! Don't spoil that! … So? … Will you help me?

| Vocabulary | | | |
|---|---|---|---|
| situation | 사태, 처지, 상황 | in fact | 사실은 |
| remember | 기억나다 | conversation | 대화 |
| last | 지난, 가장 최근의 | call | 전화하다 |
| do research (on) | (~에 대해) 조사하다 | sergeant | 경사 |
| professional | 전문적인 | (police) station | 경찰서 |
| cold | 냉정한 | certainly | 확실히, 틀림없이 |
| calculating | 계산적인 | enemy | 적 |
| far | 훨씬 | destroy | 망치다, 파멸시키다 |
| confidential | 기밀의, 비밀의 | make a mistake | 실수하다 |
| data | 자료, 데이터 | spoil | 망치다, 손상하다 |
| get back | 되찾다 | | |

Olive Green

# What should David do?

D: But if I find her ... You won't hurt her! Do you understand?

M: I'm not going to! In fact, I'm gonna ask her to work for me!

D: All right. I'll do it!

M: Use this! It's a safe phone. We must be extra careful with Miss Green. And here are the names and addresses of her former associates. Start there! And one more thing! It's sad, but your mum's got into debt. Enormous debt! Did you know that? Her little guest house can be mine even tomorrow, so ... Need I say more?

| Vocabulary | | |
|---|---|---|
| | if | 만일 ~한다면 |
| | understand | 알다, 알아듣다 |
| | ask | 부탁하다, 요청하다 |
| | safe phone | 안전한 전화기 |
| | be careful with | ~에 대해 조심하다 |
| | extra | 특별히, 각별히 |
| | former | 예전의, 과거의 |
| | associate | 동료 |
| | sad | 슬픈 |
| | get into debt | 빚을 지다 |
| | enormous | 엄청난, 막대한 |
| | little | 작은, 소규모의 |
| | guest house | 게스트하우스 |

agree

refuse

D: Forget it!

M: If you don't find her ... My friends will! And they won't be nice to her! I can promise you that!

D: All right! I'll do it!

M: Use this! It's a safe phone. We must be extra careful with Miss Green. And here are the names and addresses of her former associates. Start there! And one more thing! It's sad, but your mum's got into debt. Enormous debt! Did you know that? Her little guest house can be mine even tomorrow, so ... Need I say more?

| Vocabulary | | |
|---|---|---|
| | forget | (가능성을) 잊다, 체념하다 |
| | if | 만일 ~한다면 |
| | promise | 장담하다, 약속하다 |
| | safe phone | 안전한 전화기 |
| | be careful with | ~에 대해 조심하다 |
| | extra | 특별히, 각별히 |
| | former | 예전의, 과거의 |
| | associate | 동료 |
| | sad | 슬픈 |
| | get into debt | 빚을 지다 |
| | enormous | 엄청난, 막대한 |
| | little | 작은, 소규모의 |
| | guest house | 게스트하우스 |

# Grammar explanations

## be going to

→ 가까운 미래에 대한 계획

Olive **is going to** buy the dress on the day of the party.   Olive는 파티 당일 날 드레스를 살 것입니다.

**Are** you two **going to** visit my manor again? Tell me. I'll make preparations.
– Yes, we are. But I won't tell you when.
두 분은 제 저택을 다시 방문하실 건가요? 말씀해 주세요. 제가 준비해 놓을게요.
– 네, 그럴 거예요. 하지만 언제가 될지는 알려드리지 않을 거예요.

We **aren't going to** change the car anytime soon. This one is only a couple of months old.   저희는 당분간 차를 바꾸지 않을 거예요. 이 차는 두 달밖에 안 되었어요.

→ 이전에 내린 결정

**Are** you **going to** tell your mum what you have done, David?
– Yes, I am. I'**m not going to** lie to her.
당신이 한 일을 엄마에게 말한 건가요, David?
– 네, 그럴 거예요. 엄마에게 거짓말하지는 않을 거예요.

What **are** we **going to** do about Robert? **Are** we **going to** cooperate? – No, we are not (aren't).   Robert에 대해 어떻게 할까요? 협조할까요? – 아니요, 그러지 않을 거예요.

I'**m going to** visit my mother in California as soon as this mess is over.
저는 이 상황이 정리되는 대로 캘리포니아에 계신 어머니를 찾아뵐 거예요.

→ 사실과 근거에 기반한 예상

David **isn't going to** participate in the evening party at the Campbells'. He hasn't been invited.   David는 Campbell 저택의 저녁 파티에 참석하지 않을 거예요. 그는 초대받지 못했거든요.

**Is** Olive **going to** have a nice time in Old Berry? – Yes, she is. It's a lovely town.
Olive가 Old Berry에서 즐거운 시간을 보낼까요? – 네, 그럴 거예요. 그곳은 멋진 마을이니까요.

Jessica is up to her neck in debt. She'**s going to** lose her guest house, isn't she?
Jessica는 빚에 허덕이고 있어요. 그녀는 자신의 게스트하우스를 잃게 될 거예요, 그렇지 않나요?

## will

→ 즉흥적인 결정

Sorry, love, I can't talk now. – OK, I **will** call you later. How about 8 p.m.?
미안해요, 자기, 지금은 통화할 수 없어요. – 알았어요, 나중에 전화할게요. 오후 8시 어때요?

My car is at the garage. – Don't worry. We **will** give you a lift.
제 차가 차고에 있어요. – 걱정하지 마세요. 저희가 태워다 드릴게요.

The meeting is cancelled. – Really? I **will** go and finish my report then.
회의가 취소되었어요. – 정말인가요? 그러면 가서 보고서 작성을 끝내야겠어요.

→ 미래에 일어날 활동

The car is completely broken, so it **won't** start this time.
차가 완전히 고장 나서, 이번에는 시동도 걸리지 않을 거예요.

Olive's got the documents. She **will** contact her boss to inform him.
Olive가 문서를 입수했어요. 그녀는 보스에게 연락해서 알릴 거예요.

Sooner or later Robert and his men **will** find Olive.
조만간 Robert와 그의 부하들이 Olive를 찾아낼 거예요.

→ 의견, 바람, 기대 (*think*, *hope*, *expect*, *be sure* 등의 동사와 함께 쓰여)

It **will** be a nice day, I **think**.  화창한 날이 될 거예요, 제 생각에는.

David **expects** that she **will** give back the documents to Robert.
David는 그녀가 Robert에게 문서를 돌려줄 것이라고 기대합니다.

I'**m sure** you **will** be just fine.  저는 당신이 괜찮을 것이라고 확신해요.

→ 요청, 제안

**Will** you do me a favour?  제 부탁을 들어주시겠어요?

Oh, it's heavy. I'**ll** carry it for you.  오, 무겁군요. 제가 들어드릴게요.

**Will** you make some tea, please?  차 좀 타 줄래요?

→ 약속, 협박

I **will** catch you one day and then ...  언젠가는 당신을 잡아서…

She **will** pay me all the money back.  그녀는 저에게 돈을 전부 갚을 거예요.

We **won't** tell anyone, promise!  아무에게도 말하지 않을게요, 약속해요!

## *be going to* vs. *will*

**be going to**

→ 이전에 내린 결정(또는 계획)

I'**m going to** visit my grandpa this summer.
저는 올여름에 할아버지를 찾아뵐 거예요.

→ 사실이나 근거에 기반한 예상

It'**s going to** be a beautiful day, not a single cloud in the sky.
화창한 날이 될 거예요, 하늘에 구름 한 점 없으니까요.

**will**

→ 즉흥적인 결정

I'm a bit sleepy. I'**ll** have a cup of coffee to keep me awake.
좀 졸려요. 커피 한 잔 마시고 잠 좀 깨야겠어요.

→ 의견, 감정, 바람, 기대 등에 기반한 예상

She **will** be a good mother, I think.
그녀는 좋은 엄마가 될 거예요, 제 생각에는.

## 현재진행 Present Continuous

→ 확정된 계획

**I'm spending** my holiday in Old Berry next year.　저는 내년에 Old Berry에서 휴가를 보낼 거예요.

Robert **is having** a meeting with my people tonight at 6 o'clock.
Robert는 오늘 저녁 6시 정각에 우리 부하들과 만날 거예요.

Olive **is leaving** the UK in two days.　Olive는 이틀 후에 영국을 떠날 것입니다.

We can't meet on Friday. You **are flying** to New York then.
우리는 금요일에 만날 수 없어요. 그때 당신은 뉴욕으로 갈 거예요.

→ 확실히 일어날 일(또는 확실히 일어나지 않을 일)

Beatrice **isn't seeing** her gardener today. He's called in sick.
Beatrice는 오늘 정원사를 만나지 못할 거예요. 그가 아파서 못 온다고 전화했어요.

He **isn't coming** because he's got a severe cold.
그는 심한 감기에 걸려서 오지 않을 거예요.

We **aren't meeting** this week but the following one, according to the wall chart.
벽보에 따르면, 우리는 이번 주가 아니라 다음 주에 만날 거예요.

The party **is taking** place at 8 p.m. on Friday, 8th August.
파티는 8월 8일 금요일 오후 8시에 열릴 것입니다.


## *will* vs. *be going to* vs. 현재진행

| will | be going to | 현재진행 |
|---|---|---|
| → 즉흥적인 결정 | → 가까운 미래에 대한 계획 | → 확정된 계획 |
| → 미래에 일어날 활동 | → 이전에 내린 결정 | → 확실히 일어날 일(또는 확실히 일어나지 않을 일) |
| → 요청, 제안 | → 사실과 근거에 기반한 예상 | |
| → 의견, 감정, 바람, 기대 등에 기반한 예상 | | |

**Will** you help me? – Yes, I **will**.　도와주시겠어요? – 네, 그럴게요.

David **will** report the incident to his sergeant.　David는 경사님에게 그 사건을 보고할 것입니다.

Oh no! He **won't** report it. He must think about his mum ...
아 이런! 그는 그것을 보고하지 않을 거예요. 그는 엄마를 생각해야 하니까요…

She hopes she **will** get a few days off to recover a bit.
그녀는 조금 회복하기 위해 며칠 휴가 내기를 바라요.

What **are** you **going to** do about it? – I**'m going to** talk to my sergeant.
그것에 대해서 어떻게 할 건가요? – 저는 경사님에게 말씀드릴 거예요.

Your mum **is going to** lose her B&B. She's got into enormous debt.
당신 어머니는 B&B를 잃게 될 거예요. 엄청난 빚을 졌거든요.

Stop this noise or I**'m calling** the police.   이 소음을 멈추지 않으면 경찰을 부를 거예요.
At 6 o'clock Robert **is having** a meeting with the Russians.
6시 정각에 Robert가 러시아 사람들을 만날 것입니다.

## 소유대명사 Possessive pronouns

소유격 + 명사 ➜ 소유대명사

| my book | ➜ | **mine** | 나의 책 |
| your car | ➜ | **yours** | 당신의 차 |
| her garden | ➜ | **hers** | 그녀의 정원 |
| his painting | ➜ | **his** | 그의 그림 |
| our place | ➜ | **ours** | 우리의 집 |
| their manor | ➜ | **theirs** | 그들의 저택 |

This is **my book**. ➜ The **book** is **mine**.   이것은 제 책입니다 → 이 책은 제 것입니다.

Son, this is **your** new **car**. ➜ This **car** is **yours**.   아들아, 이것이 네 새 차다. → 이 차는 네 것이다.

The garden belongs to Beatrice. It's **her garden**. ➜ The **garden** is **hers**.
정원은 Beatrice 소유입니다. 그녀의 정원이죠. → 정원은 그녀의 것입니다.

The painting belongs to Robert. It's **his painting**. ➜ It is **his**.
그림은 Robert 소유입니다. 그의 그림이죠. → 그림은 그의 것입니다.

Don't touch it. It is the dog's bone. It's **its bone**. ➜ It is **its**.
만지지 마세요. 그것은 개의 뼈예요. 그것의 뼈죠. → 뼈는 개의 것입니다.

The only B&B in Old Berry belongs to my mum and me. It's **our place**. ➜ It is **ours**.
Old Berry의 유일한 B&B는 엄마와 제 소유예요. 우리 집이죠. → 그곳은 우리 것입니다.

Robert, you and Beatrice have a lovely private park. It is **your park**. ➜ The **park** is **yours**.
Robert, 당신과 Beatrice는 멋진 개인 정원을 가지고 있어요. 당신들의 정원이죠. → 정원은 당신들의 것입니다.

This manor belongs to the Campbells. It's **their manor**. ➜ The **manor** is **theirs**.
이 저택은 Campbell 가족 소유입니다. 그들의 저택이죠. → 저택은 그들의 것입니다.

# Communication situations

**Read the following dialogues at the travel agency.**

"Hello again. I'm sorry to have kept you waiting. It's a busy time, peak season for travel agencies. But anyway, you've had a couple of minutes to have a look at our catalogue. Have you picked a destination?"

## Dialogue 1

**Client:** No, I haven't. I'd like you to recommend a nice place to go.

**Travel agent:** Of course, no problem. A quick question then. Do you prefer to spend your holiday actively or would you like to rest and enjoy the view?

**Client:** A bit of both would be perfect.

**Travel agent:** Of course. Let me propose a package with 7 days of touring and 7 days at the seaside.

**Client:** All right. What cities are included in the touring part?

**Travel agent:** Let me check the catalogue … The main cities of Spain are mentioned. And you end the touring part in Majorca.

**Client:** You mean we'll be on a ferry.

**Travel agent:** Yes, that's exactly what I mean.

**Client:** Oh no, I suffer from seasickness.

**Travel agent:** Oh, I'm sorry to hear that. In that case you can consider the 7-day stay offer.

**Client:** What kind of hotel will I stay in?

| | |
|---|---|
| **Travel agent:** | You will be accommodated in a four-star hotel. |
| **Client:** | Are the rooms air-conditioned? |
| **Travel agent:** | Yes, they are. |
| **Client:** | OK. Could you book a single room for me, please? |
| **Travel agent:** | With a sea view? |
| **Client:** | Yes, it would be nice. |
| **Travel agent:** | OK. It's done. I'll e-mail you all the details. |

**busy** 바쁜 | **actively** 활동적으로 | **rest** 쉬다, 휴식하다 | **ferry** 페리 | **suffer from** ~을 앓다, ~로 고생하다 | **seasickness** 뱃멀미 |
**I'm sorry to hear that.** 그거 안타깝네요. | **accommodate** 숙박시키다, 공간을 제공하다 | **air-conditioned** 냉방 장치가 있는

## Dialogue 2

| | |
|---|---|
| **Client:** | Almost. I'd like to go somewhere in Europe. |
| **Travel agent:** | All right. What kind of holiday are you interested in: a self-drive holiday, honeymoon or other? |
| **Client:** | What is a self-drive holiday? |
| **Travel agent:** | It's a type of holiday where you get to your holiday destination by your own means of transport. Usually a car or a train. A plane, if not chartered, is too expensive. The accommodation and full board is included in the price. |
| **Client:** | No, that's not for me. |
| **Travel agent:** | Oh, I see. Maybe a weekend in London? |
| **Client:** | I'd rather go abroad. And I'd like to go the following weekend. |
| **Travel agent:** | May I recommend Madrid? Or Berlin? These cities are perfect for 2 or 3 nights out. |
| **Client:** | I'm taking my friends with me so maybe Berlin is a good choice. |
| **Travel agent:** | Yes, that's a very good choice. You won't regret it. |

# Vocabulary plus

**adventure** 진기한 경험, 모험

**all-inclusive** 모두 포함한

**availability** (입수) 가능성

**Brilliant!** 좋아!

**by the sea** 바닷가에

**catch cold** 감기에 걸리다

**change the criteria** 기준을 바꾸다

**convenient** 편리한, 간편한

**flexible** 탄력적인, 융통성 있는

**give up on** ~을 포기하다, 단념하다

**half board** (호텔의) 1박 2식 제공

**high-quality** 고급의

**I'm glad to hear it.** 그렇다면 다행이에요.

**in the offer** 할인 중인

**luxury suite** (호텔 객실) 럭셔리 스위트

**meet requirements** 요건을 충족하다

**package tour** 패키지 여행

**pay extra** 추가금을 지불하다

**pay in advance** 선불하다, 돈을 먼저 치르다

**play** 연극

**reclining** (등받이가) 뒤로 젖혀지는

**round** (권투 등의) 한 라운드, 한 시합, 한 경기

**satisfied** 만족한

**seaside resort** 해변 휴양지

**start from the beginning** 처음부터 다시 시작하다

**volleyball pitch** 배구 경기장

Olive Green

# Cultural tips

## Did you know that ...?

A bed and breakfast (B&B for short) is a small, private family house that offers overnight accommodation and breakfast. B&Bs are generally a perfect option for travellers with a limited budget, and a good alternative to staying at hotels. There are numerous B&Bs in seaside towns, the countryside as well as city centres.

# Scene 3 (15)     Film dialogue and vocabulary

**Read the dialogue between Jessica (J) and David (D). Check the list of words and phrases below.**

You're not wearing your uniform? You start work at 8.00 a.m.! You'll be late!

I've taken the day off.

J: The day off? Are you sick? Hangover? If it's a plain hangover … Gosh – tea and a fry-up will make you feel better. I'll fry some eggs and bacon, okay?

D: I'm not sick, it's not a hangover. I just … have an important appointment in London today. And … I need to borrow your car to get there.

J: My car? What's wrong with yours?

| Vocabulary | | | |
|---|---|---|---|
| uniform | 유니폼, 제복 | tea | 차 |
| be late | 지각하다, 늦다 | fry-up | 기름에 지진 음식으로 된 식사 |
| take the day off | 휴가 내다 | egg | 달걀 |
| be sick | 아프다 | bacon | 베이컨 |
| hangover | 숙취 | appointment | 약속 |
| plain | 단순한, 평범한 | today | 오늘 |
| Gosh! | 어이쿠! | borrow | 빌리다 |

## What should David do?

- **D:** Olive's got it!
- **J:** You mean you've lent it to her or she has stolen it?
- **D:** She's stolen it.
- **D:** Okay ... here's the thing ...
- **J:** I don't want to know! Really, I don't! ... First, you two start dating, then all of a sudden you stop! ... And you're so miserable. And I think "Okay, she's just a girl, he'll get over it! And a few days later ... You're sitting here with a silly face, your car's gone, and suddenly your work doesn't mean anything to you.
- **D:** It's more complicated than that! Mum, are you going to give me your car or not? I need to know now because the bus leaves in 20 minutes or so!
- **J:** All right, all right! ... Is she at least worth it?
- **D:** I doubt it, but I'll know soon enough!

| Vocabulary | | | |
|---|---|---|---|
| mean | 의미하다 | silly face | 멍한 얼굴 |
| lend | 빌려주다 | be gone | 없어지다, 떠나다 |
| steal | 훔치다 | suddenly | 갑자기 |
| date | 데이트하다 | bus | 버스 |
| all of a sudden | 갑자기 | at least | 적어도 |
| miserable | 비참한, 불행한 | doubt | 확신하지 못하다, 의심하다 |

**D:** It's broken ... Totally! ... It'll be the engine or ... some other part!

**J:** Your car was okay yesterday in the evening! Especially when you followed Olive to Campbell Manor.

**D:** Okay ... here's the thing ...

**J:** I don't want to know! Really, I don't! ... First, you two start dating, then all of a sudden you stop! ... And you're so miserable. And I think "Okay, she's just a girl, he'll get over it! And a few days later ... You're sitting here with a silly face, your car's gone, and suddenly your work doesn't mean anything to you.

**D:** It's more complicated than that! Mum, are you going to give me your car or not? I need to know now because the bus leaves in 20 minutes or so!

**J:** All right, all right! ... Is she at least worth it?

**D:** I doubt it, but I'll know soon enough!

| Vocabulary | | | |
|---|---|---|---|
| totally | 완전히 | miserable | 비참한, 불행한 |
| engine | 엔진 | silly face | 멍한 얼굴 |
| part | 부품 | be gone | 없어지다, 떠나다 |
| especially | 특히, 유난히 | suddenly | 갑자기 |
| follow | 뒤를 따라가다 | bus | 버스 |
| date | 데이트하다 | at least | 적어도 |
| all of a sudden | 갑자기 | doubt | 확신하지 못하다, 의심하다 |

# Grammar explanations

### 단순현재: 일정 및 계획 Present Simple: schedules and arrangements

**A:** Excuse me, I'd like to get to London. What time **does** the train **leave**?
실례합니다. 런던에 가려고 하는데요. 기차가 몇 시에 출발하나요?

**B:** It's 10 o'clock now. The train **leaves** at 10.05.   지금이 10시 정각이고요. 기차는 10시 5분에 출발합니다.

**A:** Oh, that's in 5 minutes. I won't make it. I need one a bit later.
아, 그러면 5분 뒤네요. 시간 맞춰 타지 못할 거예요. 좀 더 나중 기차를 타야겠어요.

**B:** How about around 10.30? This train **arrives** at the platform at 10.25 and **leaves** again at 10.30.   10시 30분경은 어떠세요? 이 기차는 10시 25분에 플랫폼에 도착해서 10시 30분에 다시 출발합니다.

**A:** Perfect! A return ticket, please.   완벽하네요! 왕복 티켓으로 주세요.


Olive **has got** very flexible working hours.   Olive는 근무 시간이 매우 유연합니다.

However, she **tries** to follow her own schedule.   하지만, 그녀는 자신이 정한 일정을 따르려고 노력합니다.

She **runs** every morning and **does** some exercises every other day.
그녀는 매일 아침 달리기를 하고, 하루 걸러 운동을 합니다.

On Fridays she always **calls** her mum.   금요일에는 늘 엄마에게 전화합니다.

Olive is a sociable person. She **meets** her friends regularly, or at least she **tries** to do so.
Olive는 사교성이 좋은 사람입니다. 정기적으로 친구들을 만나거나, 최소한 그렇게 하려고 노력합니다.


### 예상을 나타내는 *will/won't*

→ 어떤 일이 미래에 일어나거나 일어나지 않을 가능성이 있다고 생각할 때

Don't worry. Everything **will** be OK.   걱정하지 마세요. 다 괜찮을 거예요.

Olive has left Old Berry and she **will not** come back here again.
Olive는 Old Berry를 떠났고 다시는 이곳에 돌아오지 않을 것입니다.

David, don't drink so much coffee today. It **won't** help you.
David, 오늘은 커피를 너무 많이 마시지 말아요. 당신에게 도움이 안 될 거예요.

→ 의견, 바람, 기대를 표현할 때(*think*, *hope*, *expect*, *be sure* 등의 동사와 함께 쓰여)

I **think** it **won't** be easy to find Olive.   저는 Olive를 찾는 일이 쉽지 않을 것이라고 생각해요.

David **hopes** she **will** contact him soon.   David는 그녀가 자신에게 빨리 연락하기를 바랍니다.

He **expects** that she **will** give back the documents to Robert.
그는 그녀가 Robert에게 문서를 돌려줄 것이라고 기대합니다.

# Communication situations

**Read the following dialogues between a couple discussing their Saturday plans.**

[yawn] Coffee on Saturday morning? Thanks, honey. It's nice to start the weekend with a good cup of coffee. What are we going to do today? Have you got any plans?

### Dialogue 1

**Wife:** Don't you think our house needs a bit of cleaning?

**Husband:** Oh, I'm glad you are saying this. So, what's the deal? How are we going to share the chores?

**Wife:** I'll take care of the garden and my workshop.

**Husband:** You mean you are going to leave the house for me?

**Wife:** I have to pick up the children at 4. I won't be able to help you.

**Husband:** Oh no … I won't do everything by myself. I think I'll just do the laundry.

**Wife:** OK. Could you also load the dishwasher?

**Husband:** Yes, sure. Putting the dishes in and pressing a button is not a problem. See you around.

---

**chores** 집안일 | **workshop** 작업장 | **be able to** ~할 수 있다 | **do the laundry** 빨래를 하다, 세탁을 하다 | **See you around.** 이따 봐.

### Dialogue 2

**Wife:** I'm staying at home and reading. And you?

**Husband:** I'd love to go to that new department store in the city centre. But I guess there are some roadworks on the way and I don't know how to get there.

**Wife:** Why don't you use the satnav?

**Husband:** Don't be silly. You know I hate that device. So once more, how will I get there?

**Wife:** I think you have to go to the bridge and then take the first turn left.

**Husband:** No, no, the first turn left is closed. I'd better go straight ahead.

**Wife:** OK. Then you go along the street up to the traffic lights.

**Husband:** There is a cinema at the corner, isn't there?

**Wife:** Exactly. Turn left at the cinema.

**Husband:** Right. And then?

**Wife:** Go straight for 300 metres and the department store is on your right.

**Husband:** All right. That should be easy. Thanks.

---

**device** 장치, 기구 | **straight ahead** 곧장 앞으로 | **along the street** 길을 따라 | **traffic lights** 신호등

### Dialogue 3

**Wife:** I'm going to work a bit in the workshop.

**Husband:** What exactly are you going to do?

**Wife:** Well, the lawn mower needs repairing.

**Husband:** Yes, the whole garden needs a bit of attention.

**Wife:** I know. When I finish repairing the lawn mower, I'll rake the leaves and cut the grass.

**Husband:** That would be lovely. Will you also water it?

**Wife:** OK. Will you take care of the house in return?

**Husband:** Sure, we have a deal.

---

**lawn mower** 잔디 깎는 기계 | **rake the leaves** (갈퀴로) 낙엽을 긁어모으다 | **cut the grass** 잔디를 깎다 | **water** 물을 주다 | **in return** 대신에, 답례로 | **We have a deal.** 그렇게 하자.

# Vocabulary plus

**change the sheets** 시트를 갈다

**detour** 둘러 가는 길, 우회로

**drive crazy** 미치게 하다

**extension cord**
(전자 기기의 전선을 연장하는) 연장선, 연장 코드

**further directions** 추가 지시, 추가 방침

**have a look** 보다

**hopefully** 바라건대

**iron** 다림질하다

**make the bed** 잠자리를 정돈하다, 이불을 개다

**nail** 못

**nut** 너트, 암나사

**over the bridge** 다리 위로, 다리를 건너

**pass** 지나가다

**pegboard** 타공판(벽에 고정하여 도구들을 매달 수 있게 한 구멍 뚫린 판)

**put in order** 정돈하다, 깨끗이 하다

**scrub** 문질러 씻다

**sort out** ~을 정리하다

**take part** 참여하다

**toolbox** 공구통, 연장통

**vacuum** 진공청소기로 청소하다

**wardrobe** 옷장

**workbench** 작업대

# Cultural tips

## Did you know that ...?

The English breakfast (also called "full English breakfast", "full breakfast", "full English" or "fry-up") is a meal that usually includes bacon, sausages, eggs, and a variety of other cooked foods, such as tomatoes, mushrooms and beans, with coffee or tea. It is especially popular in the UK and Ireland, and also relatively common in other English-speaking countries.

# Scene 4 (16) — Film dialogue and vocabulary

**Read the dialogue between Olive (O) and the client (C). Check the list of words and phrases below.**

I want to deliver the thing today! Today! I could still catch an afternoon flight to the States!

C: It's not going to happen! I may need to take precautions because you messed up the job in Old Berry. The police are not doing anything, but Robert Murray may be up to something.

O: Like what?

C: There are things I haven't told you about him. For now – just find a safe place and stay there.

| | | | |
|---|---|---|---|
| deliver | 전하다, 넘겨주다 | happen | (일이) 일어나다, 생기다 |
| catch a flight | 비행기를 타다 | take precautions | 조심하다, 대책을 세우다 |
| afternoon | 오후의, 오후 | mess up | 망치다 |

**level A2**

**Read the dialogue between Olive (O) and Alfie (A). Check the list of words and phrases below.**

O: Look, I need a clean car! Nothing big, but I need it now!

A: Not a problem. You may have one of the two parked at the back. They are five grand each.

O: Five thousand of your damned British pounds? You usually take far less!

A: Yes, but I can tell that you're deep in trouble! Which for me is a great business opportunity!

O: You heartless bastard! I don't have that much cash on me!

| Vocabulary | | | |
|---|---|---|---|
| clean | 깨끗한 | British | 영국의 |
| park | 주차하다 | heartless | 매정한, 무자비한 |
| grand | 천 파운드; 천 달러 | bastard | 자식, 놈, 녀석 |
| damned | 빌어먹을 | cash | 현금, 현찰 |

# What should Olive do?

negotiate · A2-04-03

leave · A2-04-04

**O:** I could give you 2k and add the sedan parked outside.

**A:** I don't like the colour, but … All right! It's a deal! (…) Good! Business is done, so it's time for refreshments! Shall I make you some tea? Coffee? Shall I get you something to eat?

**O:** That would be great. How much for the food? A thousand quid?

**A:** Okay, okay … I'll take 2 grand and the car parked outside. (…) Good! Business is done, so it's time for refreshments! Shall I make you some tea? Coffee? Shall I get you something to eat?

**O:** That would be great. How much for the food? A thousand quid?

**Vocabulary**

| | |
|---|---|
| add | 추가하다, 보태다 |
| sedan (AmE) / saloon (BrE) | 세단형 자동차 |
| outside | 밖에, 바깥에 |
| colour | 색깔 |
| refreshments | 음료, 다과 |
| coffee | 커피 |
| quid | 1파운드 |

**Vocabulary**

| | |
|---|---|
| outside | 밖에, 바깥에 |
| refreshments | 음료, 다과 |
| coffee | 커피 |
| quid | 1파운드 |

# Grammar explanations

## 조동사: *may*    Modal verbs: *may*

→ 허가 (매우 정중한 표현)

**May** I know what went wrong? – No, you **may not**.
무엇이 잘못되었는지 알 수 있을까요? – 아니요. 그럴 수 없어요.

**May** I sit here? – Yes, you **may**.    여기에 앉아도 될까요? – 네, 그러세요.

**May** I use your car? – No, you **may not**.    당신의 차를 사용해도 될까요? – 아니요, 그럴 수 없어요.

**May** I have the keys? – Here you are.    제가 열쇠를 받아도 될까요? – 여기 있어요.

You **may** take one of the two cars parked outside.
밖에 주차되어 있는 차 두 대 중 하나를 가져가도 됩니다.

You **may** share the workshop with me.    저와 작업장을 같이 쓰셔도 됩니다.

→ 가능성 (50% 확률)

Robert **may** be up to something. I'm not sure yet.
Robert가 무슨 일을 꾸미고 있을 수도 있어요. 아직 확실하지는 않지만요.

You **may** have to hide for a while. I'll let you know.
당신은 잠시 숨어 있어야 할 수도 있어요. 제가 알려 드릴게요.

Olive needs a clean car. She **may** do some business with Alfie or she **may** go to another dodgy workshop.
Olive는 깨끗한 차가 필요해요. 그녀는 Alfie와 거래할 수도 있고 다른 수상한 작업장으로 갈 수도 있어요.

David is going to find Olive. It **may** take him only one day but it **may** also take him 3 or 4 days. He doesn't know yet.
David는 Olive를 찾을 거예요. 하루밖에 안 걸릴 수도 있지만 3~4일이 걸릴 수도 있어요. 그도 아직은 몰라요.

Robert made David track Olive down. But he is not so sure about the young policeman. He **may** have to ask the Russians for help.    Robert는 David에게 Olive를 찾아내도록 했어요. 하지만 그는 그 젊은 경찰관을 그렇게 신뢰하지 않아요. 그는 러시아인들에게 도움을 요청해야 할 수도 있어요.

| + | I/you/he/she/it/we/you/they + **may** + 동사원형 |
|---|---|
| − | I/you/he/she/it/we/you/they + **may not** + 동사원형 |
| ? | **May** + I/you/he/she/it/we/you/they + 동사원형? |
| +/− | Yes, I/you/he/she/it/we/you/they **may**.<br>No, I/you/he/she/it/we/you/they **may not**. |

She **may do** some business with Alfie or she **may go** to another dodgy workshop.
그녀는 Alfie와 거래를 할 수도 있고 다른 수상한 작업장으로 갈 수도 있어요.

David **may not find** Olive straight away.   David는 Olive를 곧바로 찾지 못할 수도 있어요.

**May** I use your car?   당신의 차를 사용해도 될까요?

May I sit here? – Yes, you **may**.   여기에 앉아도 될까요? – 네, 그러세요.

May I know what went wrong? – No, you **may not**.
무엇이 잘못되었는지 알 수 있을까요? – 아니요, 그럴 수 없어요.

## 조동사: 가정을 나타내는 *could*   Modal verbs: *could* for hypothesising

| + | I/you/he/she/it/we/you/they + **could** + 동사원형 |
|---|---|
| − | I/you/he/she/it/we/you/they + **could not (couldn't)** + 동사원형 |
| ? | **Could** + I/you/he/she/it/we/you/they + 동사원형? |
| +/− | Yes, I/you/he/she/it/we/you/they **could**.<br>No, I/you/he/she/it/we/you/they **could not (couldn't)**. |

I **could** buy the dress and then give it back to the shop. I won't need it.
Hmm, but **could** I do that? No, I **couldn't**. The lady in the shop sells dresses, she doesn't lend them out.
드레스를 산 다음에 다시 가게에 돌려줄 수 있다. 필요 없어질 테니까.
흠, 하지만 그렇게 할 수 있을까? 아니, 못 한다. 가게 점원은 드레스를 파는 거지, 빌려주는 게 아니니까.

How can I get to the building? **Could** Curtis help me?
Yes, he **could**. He **could** invite me to the party.
건물까지 어떻게 갈 수 있을까? Curtis가 나를 도와줄 수 있을까?
그래, 그럴 수 있다. 그가 나를 파티에 초대할 수도 있다.

She is such a thoughtful girl! ... But now I **could** kill her with my bare hands.
– Come on Alfie, you **couldn't** kill Olive. You are a thief, not a murderer.
그녀는 정말 자상한 여자예요! … 하지만 지금 저는 그녀를 맨손으로도 죽일 수 있어요.
– 정신 차려 Alfie, 너는 Olive를 죽일 수 없어. 너는 도둑이지 살인자가 아니라고.

It's not so bad after all. We **could** stay here without food with our mouth shut. Then we **couldn't** even talk.
어쨌든 그렇게 나쁜 건 아니에요. 우리는 여기서 음식 없이 입 닫고 지낼 수 있어요. 그다음에는 말도 할 수 없게 되겠죠.

## 조동사: 정중한 제안이나 요청을 나타내는 *shall*
### Modal verbs: *shall* for polite offers, suggestions or requests

**Would** you like some tea or coffee? **Shall** I make you some tea or coffee?
차나 커피를 드시겠어요? 차나 커피를 타 드릴까요?

**Do** you **want** something to drink? **Shall** I prepare something to drink?
마실 것을 원하시나요? 마실 것을 준비해 드릴까요?

Oops, you are in deep trouble. **Do** you **want** me to help you? **Shall** I help you?
이런, 큰 곤경에 빠지셨군요. 제가 도와 드리기를 원하시나요? 제가 도와드릴까요?

**Why don't** we have breakfast together? **Shall** we have breakfast together?
같이 아침 식사를 하는 것이 어때요? 같이 아침 식사를 할까요?

**How about** checking the car outside? **Shall** we check the car outside?
밖에 있는 차를 확인해 보는 것이 어때요? 밖에 있는 차를 확인해 볼까요?

**Why don't** we make a deal? **Shall** we make a deal?
거래를 하는 것이 어때요? 거래를 할까요?

### *shall* vs. *would like*

| shall | would like |
|---|---|
| **Shall** + I/we + 동사원형? | **Would** + you/he/she/it/they + **like** + 명사? |
| Shall we have some tea?  차 좀 마실까요? | Would you like some tea?  차 좀 드시겠어요? |
| | **Would** + you/he/she/it/they + **like to** + 동사원형? |
| | Would you like to sit down for a moment?  잠시 앉아 계시겠어요? |

level A2  Scene 4 (16)

# Communication situations

**Read the following dialogues between a TV host and one of the show's participants.**

Ladies and gentlemen, welcome after the break! You're watching Who Wants to Be Filthy Rich, season 10! Here with me is Curtis, who is going to answer his last question for £505. Curtis, are you ready?

### Dialogue 1

**Curtis:** As ready as I'll ever be!

**TV host:** Perfect. Let's start. Curtis, one kilometre equals what in miles?

**Curtis:** Imperial or nautical?

**TV host:** Oh, good catch! Imperial, of course. What's your answer, Curtis?

**Curtis:** One kilometre is equal to 0.6214 imperial miles.

**TV host:** Yes, yes! Bravo. Are you ready to go on? Let's start with the questions for £1,001. One yard: how many feet is that?

**Curtis:** One yard equals 3 feet.

**TV host:** That is correct! Bravo, Curtis! Shall we continue?

**Curtis:** Yes, I'm just warming up.

**TV host:** Good! Because the further we go, the more complicated our game becomes … Curtis, how many centimetres are there in one inch?

**Curtis:** Another maths question? That's not fair!

**TV host:** Let me remind you that all the questions are picked at random by our computer. So don't be a baby and fight! The money is waiting! And people are watching!

**Ladies and gentlemen!** 신사 숙녀 여러분! | **filthy rich** 더럽게 부자인, 더럽게 돈이 많은 | **equal** ~이다, ~와 같다 | **imperial** (도량형의) 영국 법정 표준의 | **nautical** 해상의, 항해의 | **Good catch!** 좋은 지적이네요! | **yard** 야드(길이 단위) | **warm up** 몸을 풀다, 준비 운동을 하다 | **inch** 인치 | **at random** 무작위로, 임의로

## Dialogue 2

**Curtis:** Yes. Let's go for it!

**TV host:** That's the spirit! Give us the names of four types of public transport and order them alphabetically.

**Curtis:** Subway, tram, tube, and underground.

**TV host:** Congratulations, you obviously know your alphabet well! But three out of four items on your list mean the same.

**Curtis:** That's right. Is there something wrong with it?

**TV host:** I'm not sure if I can accept this answer.

**Curtis:** Why not?

**TV host:** Oh, well. It seems that our question left too much room for interpretation.

**Curtis:** That's not really my problem. I gave you the right answer.

**TV host:** So you did. Fair enough. We'll go on with the show after a short commercial break.

**obviously** 분명히, 확실히 | **room for interpretation** 해석의 여지 | **Fair enough.** 인정합니다. / 좋아요. | **commercial** 광고 방송

## Dialogue 3

**TV host:** One yard: how many feet is that?

**Curtis:** Hmm, I'm not sure.

**TV host:** Curtis, you have 4 lifebuoys. Would you like to use one?

**Curtis:** Do you think it's time for one?

**TV host:** It's your game and your decision, Curtis. I can't make up your mind for you.

**Curtis:** I think I'll take Pester-the-People.

**lifebuoy** 구명부표 | **I can't make up your mind for you.** 제가 당신 대신 결정해 줄 수는 없어요. | **pester** 조르다, 들볶다

# Vocabulary plus

**alienate** 멀리하다, 따돌리다

**apply to** ~에 적용되다

**break the law** 법을 어기다

**confirmation of delivery** 배송 확인서

**fight well** 잘 싸우다, 선전하다

**final decision** 최종 결정

**go with the wind** 바람과 함께 사라지다

**hint** 힌트, 귀띔

**I don't have the faintest idea.** 전혀 모르겠어요.

**I haven't got a clue.** 모르겠어요.

**indecisive** 우유부단한

**of one's own free will** ~의 자유 의지로, 자발적으로

**rash** 경솔한, 성급한

**refuse** 거절하다

**round of applause** 한 차례의 박수갈채

**sign for** ~에 서명하다

**sink** 가라앉다, 침몰하다

**spirit of competition** 경쟁 열기

**technical break** 기술적 중단

**textbook** 교과서적인, 전형적인

**The show must go on.** 쇼는 계속되어야 해요.

**vote** 투표하다

# Cultural tips

## Did you know that ...?

The pound sterling (symbol: £), commonly known as the "pound", is the official currency of the United Kingdom. A common slang term for the pound is "quid". £1,000 (or: 1k) is a "grand".

# Scene 5 (17) — Film dialogue and vocabulary

**Read the dialogue between Cloutier (C) and David (D). Check the list of words and phrases below.**

"Three village girls by the stream" by Francesco Mazzini. Splendid, isn't it?

C: The beauty of the female body was his favourite topic. Oil on canvas, 70 by 50 cm. The wood frame is not original. That is why it is fairly inexpensive. Only 15 thousand pounds! You're disappointed? I understand! But you mustn't be upset! I have something less expensive you may like! It's called "The power of man"!

D: But it looks like a .... No, it is a giant ...

C: Yes! Almost two metres in height! Truly impressive! But it's made of cheap plaster! ... Now, tell me ... What do you want?

D: Olive Green! I must find her! I know you two ... worked together in the past. If you know where she is, you have to tell me!

level A2

> Two things, my young friend. First, I don't have to do anything. Second, I don't know anyone with that name.

## Vocabulary

| | | | |
|---|---|---|---|
| village | 촌락, 마을 | disappointed | 실망한 |
| splendid | 멋진 | upset | 속상한 |
| beauty | 아름다움 | expensive | 비싼 |
| female | 여성의 | power | 힘 |
| body | 육체, 몸 | giant | 아주 큰, 거대한 |
| favourite | 아주 좋아하는; 특히 잘하는 | almost | 거의 |
| topic | 주제 | metre | 미터 |
| oil | 유화 물감 | height | 높이 |
| canvas | 캔버스 | truly | 아주 |
| wood | 나무, 목재 | impressive | 인상적인 |
| frame | 액자, 틀 | cheap | 싸구려의, 값싼 |
| original | (복사본이 아닌) 진품의 | plaster | 석고 |
| fairly | 아주 | past | 과거 |
| inexpensive | 저렴한 | second | 둘째 |

# What should David do?

**D:** You're lying! I know everything about you! She stole works of art for you! Tell me where she is! You don't want me to come back here with my colleagues, do you?

**C:** Sir, I don't know anything about ... Olive Green? ... Me, working with a thief? That's a good one! I'm a respectable art dealer! Everything here is totally legal!

**D:** But I need this information!

**C:** Marco!

**D:** Look, I don't want to hurt her! I want to help her! Can you please tell me?

**C:** Sir, I don't know anything about ... Olive Green? ... Me, working with a thief? That's a good one! I'm a respectable art dealer! Everything here is totally legal!

**D:** But I need this information!

**C:** Marco!

**Vocabulary**

| lie | 거짓말하다 |
| colleague | 동료 |
| work | 작품 |
| respectable | 품위 있는, 고상한 |
| art dealer | 미술상 |
| legal | 합법적인 |

| respectable | 품위 있는, 고상한 |
| art dealer | 미술상 |
| legal | 합법적인 |

# Grammar explanations

## Have/has to vs. must

| have/has to | must |
|---|---|
| ➜ 외부 요인에 의해 어떤 것을 해야 할 때 | ➜ 스스로가 필요성이나 책임감을 느낄 때 |

Olive **has to** accept the plan. She **has to** think about her mother.
Olive는 계획을 받아들여야 해요. 어머니를 생각해야 하니까요.

It's already noon. We **have to** eat something.   벌써 정오예요. 우리는 뭔가를 먹어야 해요.

Alfie, do you **have to** keep talking all the time? It's irritating.
Alfie, 그렇게 계속 떠들어야겠니? 거슬린단 말이야.

David, don't fall in love with Olive. You **have to** remember about her real job. She's an art thief!   David, Olive를 사랑하면 안 돼요. 그녀의 진짜 직업을 기억해야 해요. 그녀는 미술품 절도범이라고요!

I **must** finish this job and leave the UK.   저는 이 일을 끝내고 영국을 떠나야 해요.

You **must** tell me!   저에게 말해야 해요!

Robert **must** find his documents or he will be in deep trouble.
Robert는 문서를 찾아야 하고 그러지 않으면 매우 곤란해질 것입니다.

## don't have to/doesn't have to vs. must not/mustn't

**don't have to/doesn't have to**

I **don't have to** tell you anything. I'll tell you if I want to.
저는 당신에게 아무것도 말할 필요가 없어요. 제가 말하고 싶으면 말할 거예요.

She **doesn't have to** buy a brand new car. She needs a clean car, that's all.
그녀는 새 차를 살 필요가 없어요. 깨끗한 차가 필요할 뿐이고, 그게 다예요.

We **don't have to** make a deal – but you need a car and I need cash.
우리는 거래를 할 필요가 없어요 – 하지만 당신은 차가 필요하고 저는 현금이 필요하죠.

**must not/mustn't**

➜ 어떤 행동이 필요하다는 내적 확신 / 금지된 것, 규칙이나 규정에 위배되는 것

You **mustn't** be upset. I'm an old man and I **mustn't** get stressed.
당신은 화내면 안 돼요. 저는 노인이라 스트레스받으면 안 되고요.

You **mustn't** shoot. That's the law.   총을 쏘면 안 돼요. 그게 법이에요.

Sir, you **mustn't** smoke here. We're at a train station.
선생님, 여기서 담배를 피우시면 안 됩니다. 우리는 기차역에 있습니다.

# Grammar explanations

## *everyone/everybody, everything, everywhere*
긍정문에서:

➜ 사람들 = **everyone/everybody**

**Everyone** at the party looked at Olive.   파티에 있던 모든 사람이 Olive를 보았습니다.

**Everybody** in Old Berry knew Jessica and her B&B.
Old Berry의 모든 사람이 Jessica와 그녀의 B&B를 알고 있었습니다.

➜ 사물들 = **everything**

**Everything** in the house was weird.   집 안의 모든 것이 이상했습니다.

In the room there was **everything** Olive needed.   방에는 Olive에게 필요한 모든 것이 있었습니다.

➜ 장소들 = **everywhere**

There was a bit of art **everywhere**.   모든 곳에 미술품이 있었습니다.

She could feel the cold in this house **everywhere**.   그녀는 이 집의 모든 곳에서 한기를 느낄 수 있었습니다.

## *someone/somebody, something, somewhere*
긍정문 및 긍정적인 대답이 기대되는 의문문에서:

➜ 사람 = **someone/somebody**

There was **somebody** in the room but she didn't know who.
방에 누군가가 있었지만, 그녀는 누구인지 몰랐습니다.

**Somebody** called Olive but she was too late to answer the phone.
누군가가 Olive에게 전화를 했지만, 그녀는 너무 늦어서 전화를 받지 못했습니다.

Did **somebody** want to talk to me? – **Yes**, it was David.
누군가가 저와 통화하고 싶어 했나요? – 네, David였어요.

➜ 사물 = **something**

I have to tell you **something**.   저는 당신에게 어떤 것을 말해야 해요.

Don't trust her. She did **something** terribly wrong.   그녀를 믿지 마세요. 그녀는 대단히 잘못된 일을 했어요.

Would you like **something** to drink? – **Yes**, some tea would be great.
마실 것 좀 드릴까요? – 네, 차 좀 주시면 좋겠어요.

Do you want to tell me **something**? – **Yes**, I've got information about Olive.
제게 뭔가를 이야기하고 싶으세요? – 네, 제가 Olive에 관한 정보를 가지고 있어요.

➜ 장소 = **somewhere**

Alfie put the keys **somewhere**. Where did he put them?
Alfie는 열쇠를 어딘가에 두었어요. 어디에 두었나요?

Where will you sleep, David? – **Somewhere** in London. I'll find a place.
어디서 잘 거예요, David? – 런던 어딘가에서요. 장소를 찾을 거예요.

Are we meeting **somewhere** in Old Berry? – **Yes**, let's meet in the park.
우리는 Old Berry 어딘가에서 만날 건가요? – 네, 공원에서 만나죠.

## no one/nobody, nothing, nowhere

긍정문에서:

→ 사람 = **no one/nobody**

She looked around. There was **nobody**. 그녀는 주위를 둘러보았습니다. 아무도 없었습니다.

Alfie, Cloutier and Marco were alone there. **No one** could hear them; **no one** could help them. Alfie, Cloutier, 그리고 Marco만이 그곳에 있었습니다. 아무도 그들의 소리를 들을 수 없었기에 아무도 그들을 도울 수 없었습니다.

→ 사물 = **nothing**

David, you can't go to the police and say: I saw **nothing**.
David, 당신은 경찰에게 가서 '아무것도 보지 못했다'고 말할 수 없어요.

What do you have in your bag? – **Nothing**. 당신 가방에 무엇이 있나요? – 아무것도 없어요.

→ 장소 = **nowhere**

I lost the map and I was going **nowhere**. 저는 지도를 잃어버려서 아무 데도 못 가고 있었어요.

I'm in deep trouble now. I don't know London and I have **nowhere** to go.
저는 지금 큰 곤경에 빠졌어요. 런던을 몰라서 갈 곳이 아무 데도 없어요.

## anybody/anyone, anything, anywhere

어떤 대답이 돌아올지 불확실한 의문문 및 부정문에서:

→ 사람 = **anybody/anyone**

Was there **anybody**? 누군가가 있었나요?

Is **anybody** home? 누군가가 집에 있나요?

She **can't** tell **anyone** in Old Berry who she really is.
그녀는 Old Berry의 누구에게도 자신이 실제로 누구인지 말할 수 없어요.

→ 사물 = **anything**

It was too late. I **couldn't** do **anything**. 너무 늦었어요. 저는 아무것도 할 수 없었어요.

Is there **anything** you could tell me about Olive? Olive에 대해 뭔가 해 줄 말이 있나요?

Is there **anything** I can help you with? 제가 뭔가 도울 수 있는 일이 있나요?

→ 장소 = **anywhere**

Where are the keys? I **can't** find them **anywhere**. 열쇠가 어디에 있죠? 어디에서도 찾을 수가 없네요.

Would you like to go **anywhere** in summer? 여름에 어딘가 가고 싶으신가요?

Did you go **anywhere** yesterday? – Yes, I did. I went to Campbell Manor.
어제 어딘가에 갔었나요? – 네, 갔어요. 저는 Campbell 저택에 갔어요.

cf. *who, what* 또는 *where*가 중요하지 않은 긍정문에서:

I can do **anything** for you: I can work for **anybody** and live **anywhere**.
저는 당신을 위해서 무엇이든 할 수 있어요: 누구 밑에서도 일할 수 있고 어디에서도 살 수 있어요.

# Communication situations

**Read the following dialogues between a client and the owner of a cabinet of curiosities.**

> It's just after 10 and we've already got a client! Good morning! Welcome to our cabinet of curiosities! What can I do for you, Sir?

### Dialogue 1

**Client:** Good morning. I'm looking for a masterpiece.

**Owner:** You've come to the right place. What kind of masterpiece are you interested in? A painting? A sculpture? Decorative arts and crafts?

**Client:** I was thinking about a painting.

**Owner:** We keep the paintings on the first floor. Let's go there. In the meantime, what kind of painting are we talking about?

**Client:** I'm interested in contemporary art.

**Owner:** Oh yes. Contemporary art is very fashionable now. What about the dimensions?

**Client:** That's not important.

**Owner:** So what are we looking for?

**Client:** I want a thought-provoking painting.

**Owner:** Fascinating! How about this one, then? It seems to be just an ordinary, white and slightly blurred spot on a black background. And yet …

---

**cabinet of curiosities** 호기심의 방 | **decorative arts and crafts** 장식 공예 | **contemporary art** 현대 미술 | **dimension** 크기, 치수; 차원 | **thought-provoking** 시사하는 바가 큰 | **blurred** 흐릿한, 희미한

### Dialogue 2

**Client:** I'm looking for traces of the past. I wonder if you have any.

**Owner:** My dear Sir, just take a look around. Everything here comes from the past. Now, what are you looking for?

**Client:** I thought about a music box.

**Owner:** I've got just the thing for you. Very old and beautiful. Have a look here.

**Client:** Are those real pearls?

**Owner:** But of course! It belonged to a duchess.

**Client:** You don't say. How do I wind it up?

**Owner:** With this tiny key. It's a luxury toy for a really special lady.

**Client:** It certainly looks pretty. What melody does it play?

**Owner:** It's no longer in working condition, I'm afraid.

**Client:** Are you saying that there is no music in the music box?

**Owner:** Unfortunately not. But I can promise you that the pearls are real and so are the gemstones on the lid.

**trace** 흔적, 자취 | **music box** 오르골 | **belong (to)** (~의) 소유물이다, (~에게) 속하다 | **wind up** (시계 따위의) 태엽을 감다 | **in working condition** 작동하는 | **gemstone** 원석 | **lid** 덮개, 뚜껑

### Dialogue 3

**Client:** I'd like to find a present for my fiancée. She loves antiquities.

**Owner:** A present for a lady! Excellent! Have you got something in mind?

**Client:** A jewellery box would be nice.

**Owner:** You're looking for a nice casket then. Let me see. What about this one?

**Client:** It's very modest. Won't impress her at all.

**fiancée** 약혼녀 | **antiquity** 골동품 | **jewellery** 보석, 장신구 | **casket** (보석 등 귀중품을 넣는) 장식함 | **modest** 수수한

# Vocabulary plus

**bolt** 빗장, 걸쇠

**bottom** (용기 안의) 바닥

**breathtaking** (너무 아름다워서) 숨이 막히는

**chain store** 체인점, 연쇄점

**china** 도자기, 사기 그릇

**clockwise** 시계 방향으로

**cog** 톱니, 이

**comfortable** 편안한

**connoisseur** (미술품이나 음식 등의) 감정가, 전문가

**depend on** ~에 달려 있다, ~에 의해 결정되다

**finger** 손가락

**gentle** 부드러운, 온화한

**grab** 붙잡다

**ground floor** 1층

**handmade** 손으로 만든, 수제의

**hard to come by** 구하기 어려운

**hidden compartment** 숨겨진 칸

**however** 하지만, 그러나

**impressed** 감동한, 감명을 받은

**instant** 순식간, 순간

**involve** 포함하다, 필요로 하다

**magnificent** 굉장히 멋진

**mantelpiece** 벽난로 위 선반

**mute** 소리를 못 내는

**neat** 교묘한, 솜씨 좋은; 깔끔한

**ornament** 장신구

**pattern** 무늬

**piece of art** 예술 작품

**pottery vase** 도자기 화병

**proceed to** ~으로 나아가다, 이동하다

**put somebody in touch with** ~와 만나게 해 주다, 연락하게 해 주다

**scratch** 긁힌 자국

**shed some light on** ~을 밝히다, ~에 해결의 실마리를 던져 주다

**specific** 구체적인, 분명한

**state-of-the-art** 최신식의, 최첨단의

**straight away** 즉시

**striking** 빼어난, 인상적인

**sublime** 탁월한, 최고의

**tear** 눈물, 울음

**the other way round** 반대로, 거꾸로

**touch** 감동시키다, 마음을 움직이다

**unconventional** 관습에 얽매이지 않는, 자유로운

**upside down** 거꾸로, 뒤집혀

**watercolour** 수채화 물감으로 그린; 수채화

**well-received** 좋은 평가를 받는, 호평을 받는

**one's own handiwork** ~가 직접 만든 수공품

# Cultural tips

## Did you know that ...?

London has many interesting museums to offer to tourists visiting the UK's capital. The top 5 might include the following: British Museum, V&A (Victoria and Albert), Natural History Museum, Science Museum and National Gallery. These and many other museums in London are open to the public for free.

The photo shows the British Museum in London.

# Scene 6 (18)      Film dialogue and vocabulary

**Read the dialogue between David (D) and Alfie (A). Check the list of words and phrases below.**

Look, she's made some enemies and now they are looking for her. I want to find her first and help her deal with the situation.

**A:** Gosh, you poor boy, you're completely clueless, aren't you? … Maybe you really wanna help her, who knows? But the fact is I haven't seen her for a long time! She came to London in August, but we couldn't meet up then. I heard that she spent some time here doing … scientific research and then flew back to the States. But that's all I know! Here's my number. Call me in a few days! I might find something out!

**D:** Thank you! You've been very helpful.

| Vocabulary | | | |
|---|---|---|---|
| completely | 완전히 | fly | (비행기를) 타고 가다 |
| clueless | 아무것도 모르는 | number | 전화 번호 |
| August | 8월 | Thank you! | 고마워요! |
| scientific | 과학의 | helpful | 도움이 되는 |

Olive Green

## What should David do?

**A:** Oh, I like this kind! It's got a fruity smell!

**D:** Look, I just want to see her! ... Please, help me mate! (...) I'm not taking this!

**A:** You don't have much choice if you really want to meet her! (...) Good boy!

| fruity | 과일 같은 |
|---|---|
| smell | 향, 냄새 |

| mate | 친구 |
|---|---|
| choice | 선택의 여지 |

# Grammar explanations

## 현재완료 vs. 단순과거 Present Perfect vs. Past Simple

**현재완료 (진행 중인 동작)**

**Olive has been in the UK for 2 weeks.**
Olive는 2주째 영국에 있습니다. (2주 전에 도착해서 지금까지 영국에 있음)

she came to the UK

**Olive hasn't finished her job yet.** Olive는 그녀의 일을 아직 못 끝냈습니다. (의뢰인에게 서류를 아직 넘기지 못 했음)

she started the job here

**Jessica has run her B&B since 2005.**
Jessica는 2005년부터 B&B를 운영 중입니다. (2005년에 열어서 현재까지 운영 중임)

2005

**David has lived in Old Berry all his life.**
David는 일생 동안 Old Berry에 살고 있습니다. (Old Berry에서 태어나서 지금까지 계속 살고 있음)

David was born

현재완료와 쓸 수 있는 시간 표현:

| for 2 days | for a month | this week | this month | this year |
|---|---|---|---|---|
| since August | since 2003 | recently | lately | yet |

### 단순과거 (종료된 동작)

**Olive was in Old Berry last week.**  Olive는 지난주에 Old Berry에 있었습니다. (지금은 Old Berry에 없음)

`last week`

**She finished her job in Old Berry.**
그녀는 Old Berry에서의 일을 끝냈습니다. (Old Berry에서의 첫 번째 임무가 끝났음)

`finished the job in Old Berry`

**Jessica ran a B&B in London for ten years, from 1995 till 2005.**  Jessica는 런던에서 10년간, 즉 1995년부터 2005년까지 B&B를 운영했습니다. (이제 런던에서 B&B를 운영하지 않으며, 2005년부터 Old Berry에서 운영 중임)

`10 years, 1995-2005`

**David stayed in London 5 years ago when he was a student.**  David는 5년 전 그가 학생일 때 런던에서 지냈습니다. (이제는 학생이 아니며 런던에서도 지내지 않음)

`stayed in London; was a student; 5 years ago`

단순과거와 쓸 수 있는 시간 표현:

| yesterday | last week/month/year | a year ago | 3 months ago | in 2003 |

### 단순과거: *would & could*   Past Simple: *would & could*

**would** = 과거에 했던 예상

**Olive wanted to go to the Campbells. She knew she would enjoy the party.**
Olive는 Campbell 저택에 가고 싶었습니다. 그녀는 파티가 재미있으리라는 것을 알았습니다.

**She couldn't stay in Old Berry. Robert would find her.**
그녀는 Old Berry에 머무를 수 없었습니다. Robert가 그녀를 찾아낼 터였습니다.

**could** = 과거에 있던 가능성

**Olive could go to the Campbells because Curtis invited her.**
Olive는 Curtis가 초대했기 때문에 Campbell 저택에 갈 수 있었습니다.

**She couldn't escape because Robert and his men found her.**
Robert와 그의 부하들이 그녀를 찾아냈기 때문에 그녀는 도망칠 수 없었습니다.

# Communication situations

**Read the following dialogues between a radio host and Jessica, a businesswoman from the town of Old Berry.**

Good morning everyone. It's Monday morning and we are about to start our weekly broadcast called "Our Local Hero". Today we host Jessica Owen, the owner of the B&B in Old Berry. She is the winner of the international contest for the best B&B in terms of service, food and hospitality. Jessica has agreed to tell us how she reached the top and what made her such a tough businesswoman. Welcome, Jessica, and thanks for joining us. Let's talk about your background first.

## Dialogue 1

| | |
|---|---|
| **Jessica:** | Hello Tom, good morning, everyone. What would you like to start with? |
| **Radio host:** | Let's talk about your childhood and school years first. |
| **Jessica:** | Well, I was actually born in Old Berry. |
| **Radio host:** | So you are very local. |
| **Jessica:** | Yes, I am. I also completed most of my school education in Old Berry. |
| **Radio host:** | Apart from the vocational school, right? |
| **Jessica:** | Yes. For that I went to Edinburgh. |
| **Radio host:** | Why did you choose a place so far away from home? |
| **Jessica:** | I knew I wouldn't have another chance to leave the town for so long. |
| **Radio host:** | Were you right? |
| **Jessica:** | I was a bit homesick at the beginning but it was a good decision. |
| **Radio host:** | And that's all for now. We'll speak again soon. Stay tuned. |

**broadcast** 방송 | **reach the top** 정상에 오르다, 최고의 지위에 오르다 | **complete** 끝내다, 완료하다 | **vocational school** 직업학교 | **be homesick** 고향을 그리워하다, 향수병을 앓다 | **Stay tuned.** 채널을 고정해 주세요.

## Dialogue 2

**Radio host:** Jessica, you've been running a family business for more than 20 years now. How did it all start?

**Jessica:** After the secondary school I went to college for vocational training.

**Radio host:** And your college was in a much bigger city.

**Jessica:** Yes, and then I went to the USA for a year.

**Radio host:** OK. That must have been a great experience. I'm sure you came back equipped with useful knowledge and all ready to work.

**Jessica:** Oh yes! I came back with my head full of ideas.

**Radio host:** And what happened?

**Jessica:** I started to work for an international company.

**Radio host:** Was it a good time in your life?

**Jessica:** Yes. In the end I became a member of the top management.

**Radio host:** OK, Jessica, let's have a short commercial break now. Stay with us.

**college** 대학, 칼리지 | **equipped with** ~을 갖춘

## Dialogue 3

**Jessica:** OK, sure. I'm ready.

**Radio host:** So, in a nutshell. After you graduated from the secondary school, you continued your education at the vocational college. Then you had a gap year and came back to work in a corporation. But your life has not always been easy.

**Jessica:** Well, I always try to look on the bright side of life.

**in a nutshell** 간단히 말해서 | **graduate** 졸업하다 | **look on the bright side of life** 인생의 밝은 면을 보다

# Vocabulary plus

**ancient** 아주 오래된

**arsonist** 방화범

**attend** (학교 등에) 다니다

**average** 평범한

**bully** 괴롭히다

**cause** 일으키다

**collapse** 무너지다, 붕괴하다

**fall in love** 사랑에 빠지다

**fire** 화재, 불

**flood** 홍수

**full-time** 풀타임으로, 전임으로

**get bored** 싫증을 내다

**hands-on experience** 실무 경험

**I'd rather not talk about it.** 별로 말하고 싶지 않아.

**in a heartbeat** 생각해 볼 것도 없이 당장

**in one's twenties** 20대에

**nursery school** 유아원

**pass on** ~을 전하다

**presumably** 아마, 짐작건대

**properties** 건물, 소유지, 부동산

**pupil** (어린) 학생

**raise** 키우다, 기르다

**redecorate** 실내 장식을 새로 하다

**rental** 집세, 임대료

**resign** 사임하다, 사직하다

**split up (with)** (~와) 헤어지다

**start from scratch** 처음부터 다시 시작하다

**start over** 처음부터 다시 시작하다

**storm** 폭풍, 폭풍우

**travel** 여행하다

**travel agent** 여행사 직원

**turn out** ~인 것으로 드러나다, 밝혀지다

**ups and downs** 기복, 상승과 하락

**wear glasses** 안경을 쓰다

# Cultural tips

## Did you know that ...?

The country code is +44 for UK phone numbers and +1 for U.S. phone numbers. Mobile phone numbers have 10 digits, and these may be preceded with an additional 0 in the UK.

# Scene 7 (19) — Film dialogue and vocabulary

**Read the dialogue between Alfie (A) and Olive (O). Check the list of words and phrases below.**

I'm having second thoughts about tea. Let's have some coffee instead, huh? There is a long night ahead of us.

You're not killing him!

**A:** Yes, I am! … I may have a few biscuits, but I'm not sharing, because they are my favourite! Be rational! He's a cop and a pain in the arse! He knows too much about you and me. Also, I'm jealous of him – you clearly have a soft spot for that moron!

**O:** I do not have a soft spot for him … or anyone else. He may be a moron, but you mustn't kill him!

**A:** Why? You're being too emotional about this! Feelings are one of women's weak points!

**O:** Alfie, no!

**A:** But that's my gun! Where did you find it?

**O:** In the loo. There are guns hidden all over this place! You're obsessed!

**D:** Guys! Turn around!

**A:** It's only one man! We can deal with that, can't we, luv?

# level A2

> Not quite, *mes amis*! Not quite!

## Vocabulary

| | | | |
|---|---|---|---|
| have second thoughts | 생각이 바뀌다 | have a soft spot for | ~에게 호감이 있다, ~에게 약하다 |
| instead | 대신에 | moron | 멍청이 |
| be ahead of | ~을 앞두고 있다 | be emotional about | ~에 감정적이다 |
| biscuit | 비스킷 | feeling | 정, 감정 |
| share | 나누어 주다 | weak point | 약점 |
| rational | 이성적인, 합리적인 | loo | 화장실 |
| cop | 경찰 | hide | 숨기다 |
| pain in the arse | 골칫거리, 아주 귀찮은 것 | be obsessed (with) | (~에) 강박이 있다, 집착하다 |
| also | 게다가, 또한 | guys | (남녀 상관없이) 사람들 |
| be jealous of | ~을 질투하다, 시기하다 | turn around | 돌아서다, 몸을 돌리다 |
| clearly | 분명히, 확실히 | | |

# Grammar explanations

## 현재진행: 상태동사 Present Continuous: state verbs

→ 일부 상태동사(*be, have, like, enjoy*)는 현재진행으로 쓸 수 있으나, 이때 의미는 달라진다:

David **is** a nice guy.   David는 착한 남자입니다. (일반적인 상태)
David **is being** aggressive today.   David는 오늘 공격적입니다. (일시적인 행동)

Alfie **has** got many cars in his workshop.
Alfie는 작업장에 차가 많이 있습니다. (소유라는 일반적인 상태를 나타냄)
Alfie **is having** second thoughts.
Alfie는 다시 한번 생각하고 있습니다. (소유가 아니라 일시적인 행동을 나타냄)

I don't **enjoy** parties. There are usually too many people there.
저는 파티를 좋아하지 않습니다. 보통 파티에는 사람이 너무 많습니다. (일반적인 상태)
I'**m enjoying** your party, Mrs Campbell. It's really nice.
저는 당신의 파티를 즐기고 있어요, Campbell 씨. 정말 멋지네요. (일시적인 행동)

Olive is a girl from New York. She **likes** big cities.
Olive는 뉴욕 출신 여자입니다. 그녀는 대도시를 좋아합니다. (일반적인 상태)
Olive is now in Old Berry – a small and nice town. She **is liking** it more than she expected.
Olive는 현재 Old Berry에 있습니다 – 작고 멋진 도시입니다. 그녀는 생각보다 그곳이 마음에 듭니다. (일시적인 행동이나 상황)

## 셀 수 있는 명사와 셀 수 없는 명사 Countable and uncountable nouns

셀 수 있는 명사

a bottle, a chair, two candles, three plates

**1.** a/an

Would you like **a biscuit**? – No, thank you.   비스킷 하나 드시겠어요? – 아뇨, 괜찮아요.
Olive has got **a problem** with David. Why has he followed her?
Olive는 David와 문제가 하나 있습니다. 그는 왜 그녀를 미행했나요?
It's going to be **an interesting night**.   흥미로운 밤이 될 거예요.

**2.** the

Where is **the bottle**? – It's on the table.   병이 어디에 있나요? – 탁자 위에 있어요.

**3.** 1, 2, 3 ...

There are **two** clean **cars** outside. You may take one of them.
밖에 깨끗한 차가 두 대 있어. 둘 중 한 대를 가져가도 좋아.

Olive has already met **two friends** in London: Alfie and Cloutier. Well, they are not real **friends**. They are her former **co-workers**.
Olive는 런던에서 벌써 친구를 둘이나 만났습니다: Alfie와 Cloutier죠. 음, 그들은 진짜 친구들은 아닙니다. 예전 동업자들이죠.

It's only **one man**. We can deal with it, can't we, love?
겨우 한 놈이잖아! 우리가 처리할 수 있지, 안 그래, 자기?

### 셀 수 없는 명사

soup, wine, water, bread, butter, meat

**1.** a/an ➜ some, 무관사

Could you give me **some water**, please?   물 좀 주시겠어요?

Would you like something to drink? – Yes, **some coffee**, please.
마실 것을 드릴까요? – 네, 커피 좀 주세요.

Let's have **some fun**!   신나게 놀아봅시다!

**Help** is on the way.   도와주러 오고 있어요.

**2.** the

Where is **the wine**? – It's on the table.   와인이 어디에 있죠? – 탁자 위에 있어요.

I need **the information** now!   당장 정보가 필요해요!

**3.** 1, 2, 3 ... ➜ a piece of, a glass of, 2 cups of 등

Tea, coffee? – **A cup of coffee**, please.   차 드실래요, 커피 드실래요? – 커피 한 잔 주세요.

There are **two bottles of water** in the fridge. Don't buy any more.
냉장고에 물이 두 병 있어요. 더는 사지 마세요.

Which would you like: red wine or white wine? – **A glass of** red **wine**, please.
어떤 것으로 드릴까요: 레드 와인 아니면 화이트 와인? – 레드 와인 한 잔 주세요.

## many/much

| many | much |
|---|---|
| eggs, trees, photos, bottles, pieces | wine, bread, information, money/cash, water |

**?**

**How many brothers** have you got?  남자 형제가 몇 명인가요?
**How many people** are there?  그곳에 사람이 몇 명 있나요?
**How many computers** do you need in your office?  사무실에 컴퓨터가 몇 대 필요한가요?

**How much money** have you got?  돈이 얼마나 있나요?
**How much bread** do we need?  빵이 얼마나 필요한가요?
**How much time** do you have for the exam?  시험 시간이 얼마나 되나요?

**−**

I don't have **many days** off.  저는 휴가 일수가 많지 않아요.
There weren't **many restaurants** in that holiday resort.  그 휴양지에는 식당이 많지 않았어요.
He's not very sociable. He doesn't have **many friends**.
그는 그다지 사교적이지 않아요. 친구가 많지 않아요.

The police don't have **much information** about the incident at the Campbells'.
경찰은 Campbell 저택에서 일어난 사건에 대한 정보를 많이 가지고 있지 않아요.
We don't have **much time** to finish the project.  우리는 프로젝트를 끝낼 시간이 많지 않아요.
There isn't **much space** left for your belongings.  당신의 소지품이 들어갈 공간이 많이 남아 있지 않아요.

### 셀 수 없는 명사 → 셀 수 있는 명사

**How much wine** do we have for the evening?  저녁에 마실 와인이 얼마나 있나요?
→ **How many bottles of wine** do we have for the evening?  저녁에 마실 와인이 몇 병 있나요?

**How much water** shall I prepare?  물을 얼마나 준비할까요?
→ **How many glasses of water** shall I prepare?  물을 몇 잔이나 준비할까요?

**How much information** has been released?  정보가 얼마나 누설되었나요?
→ **How many pieces of information** have been released?  정보가 몇 가지나 누설되었나요?

cf. *a lot of*는 셀 수 있는 명사와 셀 수 없는 명사에 모두 사용된다.

There are **a lot of things** to do in Old Berry.  Old Berry에는 할 것이 많아요.
There is **a lot of wine** left.  와인이 많이 남았어요.

# Communication situations

**Read the following dialogues between Jessica and David planning to replenish the food for their B&B in Old Berry.**

Good news, David! We are fully booked for the month. Now, we have to prepare for hosting so many people. I have to have food in stock.

### Dialogue 1

**David:** That's great news, mum.

**Jessica:** I know! And so I need your help in the kitchen.

**David:** I can go shopping and buy things in bulk.

**Jessica:** That's exactly what you are going to do. Here is the list.

**David:** OK. Let me see.

**Jessica:** Can you read my handwriting?

**David:** A bag of carrots, canned peas and beans, and spinach.

**Jessica:** OK. And I need fresh spinach. Not frozen and not canned, remember!

---

**host** 접대하다 | **in stock** 비축하여, 재고로 | **great news** 정말 좋은 소식 | **in bulk** 대량으로 | **handwriting** 글씨 | **bag** 봉지; 가방 | **carrot** 당근 | **canned** 통조림으로 된 | **peas** 완두콩 | **beans** 콩 | **spinach** 시금치

### Dialogue 2

**David:** You could try sushi. It's very popular now.

**Jessica:** Oh David, I'm too old for that. And I prefer traditional British cuisine.

**David:** You mean bacon and eggs? And fried sausages?

**Jessica:** Don't be mean, David. I cook for my guests, not for you. Actually, why don't you start cooking for yourself if you dislike my food so much?

---

**traditional** 전통의, 전통적인 | **cuisine** 요리 | **sausage** 소시지 | **cook** 요리하다

**level A2** Scene 7 (19)

# Vocabulary plus

**bar of soap** 비누 한 조각
**be off the hook** 곤경을 면하다
**beef** 소고기
**beetroot** 비트
**brand** 상표, 브랜드
**bread** 빵
**butcher** 정육점
**cheese on toast** 치즈 얹은 토스트
**chop** 잘게 썰다
**clove of garlic** 마늘 한 쪽
**cod** (어류) 대구
**coffee machine** 커피 머신
**cucumber** 오이
**delicious** 아주 맛있는
**dish** 요리
**drag one's heels** 꾸물거리다
**drink-driving** 음주 운전
**duck** 오리
**feel like** ~이 먹고/갖고/하고 싶다
**fill up** ~을 채우다
**firstly, ... secondly, ...** 첫째로, … 둘째로, …
**fish** 물고기, 생선
**for the record** 참고로; 분명히 말하는데
**freeze** 얼리다
**French fries** 프렌치프라이
**global village** 지구촌
**Good for you.** 잘됐네요.
**grilled chicken** 구운 닭고기
**herbs and spices** 허브와 향신료

**homeless shelter** 노숙자 쉼터
**illegible** 읽기 어려운
**ingredient** 재료
**inspire** 영감을 주다
**instant** 인스턴트의
**It's high time (that) ...** ~을 해야 할 때다
**lamb** 양고기, 양
**large** (규모가) 큰, (양이) 많은
**latecomer** 지각자, 늦게 오는 사람
**lobster** 랍스터
**medium** 중간의
**mint sauce** 민트 소스
**olive** 올리브
**on the line** 통화 중인
**onion** 양파
**pantry** 식료품 저장실
**parsley** 파슬리
**patty** 패티(다진 고기를 동글납작하게 빚은 것)
**peel** 껍질을 벗기다
**peeler** 껍질 벗기는 칼
**police station** 경찰서
**pork** 돼지고기
**potato** 감자
**prawn** 참새우
**pumpkin** 호박
**rabbit** 토끼
**raw** 날것의, 익히지 않은
**recipe** 요리법, 조리법
**salad** 샐러드

**season** 계절
**serve** 제공하다
**set** 세트
**shrimp** 새우
**slice** 얇게 저미다
**smoked salmon** 훈제 연어
**soda** 탄산음료
**sole** (어류) 서대기
**stink out** 악취를 풍기다
**stir** 젓다
**supplier** 공급업자
**take a risk** 모험을 하다
**takeaway** 테이크아웃 음식
**tasty** 맛있는
**the tip of the iceberg** 빙산의 일각
**thought** 생각
**to go** (식당에서 먹지 않고) 가지고 갈
**ton** 다량, 아주 많음; 톤
**Tough luck.** 안타깝네. / 운도 없지.
**tuna** 참치
**turkey** 터키
**veal** 송아지 고기
**veggie** 채식주의자의
**watch oneself** 신중히 행동하다, 자제하다
**What were you thinking?** 대체 무슨 생각이니?
**What's the big deal?** 그게 무슨 대수야?

# Cultural tips

## Did you know that ...?

"Tea at 5 o'clock in the afternoon" may be a stereotype, because British people actually drink tea at every hour of the day. A cup of tea (informally called "a cuppa") is almost a symbol of the British culture, especially if it is accompanied by some cake or biscuits. British people nearly always put milk in their tea.

## Scene 8 (20) — Film dialogue and vocabulary

Read the dialogue between Olive (O), Cloutier (C) and Alfie (A).
Check the list of words and phrases below.

How did you know where I am?

A2-08-01

C: Marco was following your friend around all day.
A: I told you he was a moron. Who are they?
O: Alfie, meet Mr Cloutier, an art dealer. He was my business partner a couple of years ago.
C: A business partner? You ungrateful girl! I taught you everything you know about stealing art. I introduced you to my clients. I invested a fortune in you!
O: I paid it all back! For years I was stealing for you and you were paying me peanuts! I made you a rich man!
C: Then you betrayed me! You took nearly all my clients! ... And I'm here to kill you for that!
O: Good luck, you two-faced fraud!
A: Alfie! Can I call you Alfie? In my car there's a suitcase with 50,000 pounds in it! It can be yours! But you have to help me kill Olive and her friend!
O: Come on, Alfie! I'll get you much more money in a couple of days ...
C: Maybe she will or maybe she won't. But I've got cash! Lots of good old cash that I can give you now!
O: Alfie, don't listen to him! Think about our special friendship!

## level A2

**Vocabulary**

| | | | |
|---|---|---|---|
| business partner | 동업자 | rich | 부유한, 돈 많은 |
| year | 1년 | betray | 배신하다 |
| ago | 전에 | nearly | 거의 |
| ungrateful | 배은망덕한, 은혜를 모르는 | Good luck! | 잘해 봐! / 행운을 빌어! |
| teach | 가르치다 | two-faced | 두 얼굴의, 위선적인 |
| introduce | 소개하다 | fraud | 사기꾼 |
| client | 고객, 의뢰인 | suitcase | 여행 가방 |
| invest | 투자하다 | in a couple of days | 며칠 뒤에 |
| fortune | 큰돈, 거금 | listen | (귀 기울여) 듣다 |
| pay back | (빌린 돈을) 갚다 | friendship | 우정 |
| pay peanuts | 푼돈을 주다 | | |

## What should Alfie do?

A: Sorry Olive, we both know that there is no "special friendship" between us. Drop the gun or he dies.

A: The answer is "no". I can kill him, but not Olive.

C: I understand! But, Alfie, think again! There are people following her … people who know who you are and what you do. You must understand that Olive's a problem now! You don't want to lose … all this!

A: The man's right! I'm sorry, Olive, our special friendship is over. Drop the gun or he dies!

| die | 죽다 |
|---|---|

# Grammar explanations

## 과거진행 Past Continuous
➡ 과거에 진행 중이던 동작
➡ 과거의 일시적인 동작

**Jessica:** Where were you all day yesterday? I called you many times.
어제 하루 종일 어디에 있었니? 내가 몇 번이나 전화했는데.

**David:** I was at work.
일하고 있었어요.

**Jessica:** At work? At 5 p.m.?
일하고 있었다고? 오후 5시에?

**David:** At 5 p.m. I **was** driv**ing** to meet somebody.
오후 5시에요. 누구 좀 만나러 가려고 운전하고 있었어요.

**Jessica:** Somebody from work?
일 때문에 만난 사람이야?

**David:** Yes, mum. We **were** work**ing** on a difficult case last week, remember?
네, 엄마. 우리가 지난주에 어려운 사건을 처리하고 있었잖아요. 기억나요?

**Jessica:** Oh, yes. And at 7 p.m.? I called you at 7. **Were** you still chatt**ing** with your colleague?
아, 그랬지. 그러면 오후 7시에는? 내가 7시에도 전화했는데. 그때도 동료와 수다 떨고 있었니?

**David:** No, I wasn't. I **was** hav**ing** a meeting with Olive.
아니요, 그러고 있지 않았어요. 저는 Olive를 만나고 있었어요.

**Jessica:** With Olive? But she went out with Curtis!
Olive를? 하지만 그 애는 Curtis와 데이트했잖아!

**David:** OK. At 7 p.m. I **was** follow**ing** her …
맞아요. 오후 7시에 저는 그녀의 뒤를 밟고 있었어요…

### 긍정문과 부정문

| | |
|---|---|
| **+** | I/he/she/it + **was** + 동사 + -ing |
| | you/we/they + **were** + 동사 + -ing |
| **−** | I/he/she/it + **wasn't (was not)** + 동사 + -ing |
| | you/we/they + **weren't (were not)** + 동사 + -ing |

**+**

She had an earphone. She **was** talk**ing** to her boss all the time.
그녀는 이어폰을 가지고 있었어요. 그녀는 내내 자신의 보스와 통화하고 있었어요.

Olive **was** runn**ing** with David yesterday morning around 8 a.m.
Olive는 어제 오전 8시쯤에 David와 달리기를 하고 있었어요.

The whole week was terrible. We **were** work**ing** hard every day.
일주일 내내 끔찍했어요. 우리는 매일 힘든 일을 하고 있었어요.

**–**

I **wasn't** follow**ing** you. I just knew you would be here.
저는 당신을 미행하고 있지 않았어요. 저는 그냥 당신이 여기에 있을 줄 알았죠.

David, I think you **weren't** hav**ing** a meeting with your colleague at 7. Am I right?
David, 나는 네가 7시에 동료와 만나고 있지 않았다고 생각해. 내 말이 맞니?

David wanted to talk to Olive but she **wasn't** listen**ing**.
David는 Olive와 이야기하고 싶었지만 그녀는 듣고 있지 않았어요.

**의문문과 대답**

| ? | **Was** + I/he/she/it + 동사 + **-ing** |
| | **Were** + you/we/they + 동사 + **-ing** |
| +/– | **Yes**, I/he/she/it **was**. / **Yes**, you/we/they **were**. |
| | **No**, I/he/she/it **wasn't** (was not). / **No**, you/we/they **weren't** (were not). |

**?**

What **were** you do**ing** yesterday at 5? I called you then.
어제 5시에 무엇을 하고 있었니? 내가 그때 전화했어.

**Was** he scann**ing** Olive's files in her room?
그가 Olive의 방에서 그녀의 파일을 살펴보고 있었나요?

How did you know I was there? **Were** you follow**ing** me all evening?
제가 그곳에 있다는 것을 어떻게 알았나요? 저녁 내내 제 뒤를 밟았나요?

**+/–**

Was David listening to Olive and Curtis? – **Yes**, he **was**.
David가 Olive와 Curtis의 말을 듣고 있었나요? – 네, 그랬어요.

Were they talking about the painting? – **Yes**, they **were**.
그들이 그림에 대해 이야기하고 있었나요? – 네, 그랬어요.

Was Jessica shouting at David in the morning? – **No**, she **wasn't**.
오전에 Jessica가 David에게 소리 지르고 있었나요? – 아니요, 그러지 않았어요.

Were they dancing at the party? – **No**, they **weren't**.
그들이 파티에서 춤추고 있었나요? – 아니요, 그러지 않았어요.

# 과거진행 vs. 단순과거 Past Continuous vs. Past Simple

### 과거진행

➜ 과거에 진행 중이던 동작

At 2 p.m. Olive **was** driv**ing** to Old Berry.   오후 2시에 Olive는 차를 몰고 Old Berry로 가고 있었습니다.

Two days later, between 10 and 11 a.m. she **was** look**ing** around to find a nice dress for the party.   이틀 후, 오전 10시에서 11시 사이에 그녀는 파티에서 입을 멋진 드레스를 찾기 위해 둘러보고 있었습니다.

➜ 과거 사건의 배경

It was a nice day. The birds **were** sing**ing** and the sun **was** shin**ing** …
멋진 날이었습니다. 새들은 노래하고 태양은 빛나고 있었습니다…

In the pub there **was** some music play**ing**. We couldn't hear each other.
술집에서는 음악이 나오고 있었습니다. 우리는 서로의 말을 들을 수 없었습니다.

### 단순과거

➜ 과거에 종료된 동작

Olive **drove** to Jessica's B&B.   Olive는 차를 몰고 Jessica의 B&B에 갔습니다.

She **bought** a dress.   그녀는 드레스를 샀습니다.

➜ 과거에 순서대로 일어난 동작

She **opened** the safety deposit box, **took** the confidential documents and **ran away**.
그녀는 금고를 열고, 기밀 문서를 꺼내 달아났습니다.

Olive and David **went out** together. They **visited** a pub, **played** pool a bit and **came back**. The date **was** over.
Olive와 David는 데이트를 했습니다. 그들은 술집에 가서, 포켓볼을 조금 치다가 돌아왔습니다. 데이트가 끝났습니다.

### 과거진행 + 단순과거

→ 더 오래 지속된 동작(과거진행, *while*)이 더 짧게 지속된 동작(단순과거, *when*)의 배경이 될 때

Olive **was looking** for a dress when the shop assistant **noticed** her.
매장 직원이 Olive를 의식했을 때 그녀는 드레스를 찾고 있었습니다.

Robert **was drinking** coffee when David **woke up**.
David가 깨어났을 때 Robert는 커피를 마시고 있었습니다.

Her boss **changed** the plan while she **was preparing** herself to steal the painting.
그녀가 그림 훔칠 준비를 하는 도중에 그녀의 보스는 계획을 바꾸었습니다.

Marco **came in** while Olive and Alfie **were talking**.
Olive와 Alfie가 이야기하는 도중에 Marco가 들어왔습니다.

# Communication situations

**Read the following dialogues between Olive and Jessica sharing unusual stories during a power cut.**

Another storm, another power cut. No television and no Internet. So, shall we play "true stories" again? It really made the time fly last week.

### Dialogue 1

**Jessica:** Sure! I'd love to share my great grandmother's story with you.
**Olive:** Great, I love family sagas. Especially if they really happened.
**Jessica:** She was born in 1895 in a small town near London.
**Olive:** I can feel it's going to be gloomy.
**Jessica:** It was a poor and large family. She was the youngest of nine.
**Olive:** Dear me! That's an odd number of children, in more ways than one.
**Jessica:** Wait. One day a circus came to town.
**Olive:** A circus? Wow! And?
**Jessica:** The circus director promised her family a lot of money for her.
**Olive:** But her parents didn't agree, did they?
**Jessica:** No, but then the circus people kidnapped her.
**Olive:** Oh no! That's terrible! How old was she?
**Jessica:** About six. Luckily she managed to escape on the second day.
**Olive:** What a smart and brave little girl! But that's a really terrifying story!

**power cut** 정전 | **fly** (시간이) 빨리 가다, 빨리 흐르다 | **gloomy** 음울한; 우울한, 침울한 | **odd** 특이한, 이상한 | **kidnap** 유괴하다, 납치하다 | **terrible** 끔찍한, 무시무시한 | **brave** 용감한 | **terrifying** 무서운

## Dialogue 2

**Jessica:** Actually, I would love to tell you what happened to me yesterday.

**Olive:** Oh yes? Good, let's hear it.

**Jessica:** As usual on Friday afternoon, I was doing the shopping …

**Olive:** … and then you heard something strange …

**Jessica:** Oh, stop it! I heard a man calling me.

**Olive:** A mysterious - and hopefully handsome - stranger appears! Go on.

**Jessica:** I ignored him at first but he kept calling me.

**Olive:** Weren't you worried at that point? That guy was as stubborn as a mule. What did you do?

**Jessica:** I finally stopped and asked: Why are you following me?

**Olive:** And how did he react?

**Jessica:** He smiled and said: "Madam, you've taken my trolley".

**Olive:** Oh no! How embarrassing! Lucky he was a gentleman about it, though.

**mysterious** 신비로운, 비밀스러운 | **handsome** 잘생긴, 멋진 | **stranger** 낯선 사람 | **appear** 나타나다 | **as stubborn as a mule** 고집불통인 | **trolley** (슈퍼마켓 등의) 카트, 손수레 | **How embarrassing!** 창피해라!

# Vocabulary plus

**against one's will** ~의 의지와 상관없이

**allow** 허락하다, 허가하다

**arrange** 마련하다, 주선하다, 준비하다

**awful** 끔찍한, 보기 흉한

**barely** 거의 ~않다

**behind one's back** ~ 몰래

**Better safe than sorry.** 나중에 후회하는 것보단 조심하는 게 낫지.

**break out** 발발하다, 발생하다

**charming smile** 매력적인 미소

**confused** 혼란스러워하는

**creepy** 소름끼치는, 오싹한

**dream of** ~을 꿈꾸다

**enchanted** 넋을 잃은, 반한

**except for** ~을 제외하고

**fairy tale** 동화

**fiancé** 약혼자(남자)

**frog** 개구리

**gesture** 몸짓, 동작

**give back** 돌려주다

**hold at gunpoint** 총구를 들이대다, 위협하다

**How come?** 어째서? / 왜?

**interrupt** 가로막다, 방해하다, 중단하다

**miss** 그리워하다

**mouths to feed** 부양 가족, 먹여 살려야 할 사람

**noble** 숭고한, 고결한

**of sorts** 불완전하나마 ~라고 할 수 있는 것

**open-minded** 편견 없는, 포용력 있는

**painful** 고통스러운, 괴로운

**patience** 인내심, 참을성

**peasant** 소작농

**pick up** ~을 들어올리다

**prince-charming** 백마 탄 왕자, 완벽한 남자

**put together** 합하다

**reunite** 재회하다

**ride horses, ride a horse** 말을 타다

**run away** 도망치다

**scared** 무서워하는, 겁먹은

**school outing** 학교 소풍, 학교 견학

**school sweetheart** 학교 때 애인

**smile broadly** 활짝 웃다

**spill the beans** (비밀을) 무심코 말해버리다

**start a family** 첫아이를 보다

**stepsister** 이복 자매

**teenager** 십대

**terrified** 겁에 질린, 몹시 무서워하는

**unpleasant** 기분 나쁜, 무례한

**unusual** 이상한, 별난

**Watch it, you.** 잘 봐 둬, 당신. / 조심해, 당신.

**When the power is back ...** 전기가 다시 들어오면…

**world-famous** 세계적으로 유명한

# Cultural tips

## Did you know that ...?

**Wages** are a type of payment a person gets for work done for a job. The amount may be fixed for a task or it may be based on time. Wages are usually paid by the hour. Work for wages is the most common form of work.

A **salary** is a type of payment a person gets for work done for a job. A salary is usually paid for a fixed period of time, like a month or a week. Generally, it does not matter how many hours are worked, the salary remains the same.

# Scene 9 (21)    Film dialogue and vocabulary

Read the dialogue between Alfie (A) and Cloutier (C).
Check the list of words and phrases below.

So grateful for the jacket, David!

**A:** You know, it's hard these days to find a good place for burying bodies in England. This one's quite popular. Many graves have been dug here! But most of them have been prettier than that one! Look, a proper grave is dug to a depth of 5 feet or more. If it is too shallow, then the body is usually found by the police, or local residents, or even wild animals.

**C:** Are they ready?

**A:** Yeah … I guess.

**C:** Damn! I can't do it! I don't do this very often, okay? Just give me five minutes alone!

**A:** Wait! I've basically quit smoking, but I could have one …

# level A2

**Vocabulary**

| | | | |
|---|---|---|---|
| grateful | 고마워하는, 감사하는 | foot | 피트(길이의 단위) |
| jacket | 재킷 | shallow | 얕은 |
| hard | 어려운, 힘든 | resident | 주민, 거주자 |
| bury | 묻다, 매장하다 | wild animal | 야생동물 |
| popular | 인기 있는 | often | 자주 |
| grave | 무덤 | Wait! | 잠깐만요! |
| dig | 파다 | basically | 원래, 기본적으로 |
| proper | 제대로 된, 적절한 | quit | 끊다, 그만두다 |
| depth | 깊이 | smoke | 담배를 피우다 |

**Read the dialogue between Olive (O) and David (D).
Check the list of phrases below.**

O: David! Now!
D: With pleasure!

With pleasure! 기꺼이!

level A2  Scene 9 (21)

# Grammar explanations

## 수동태: 단순현재 & 현재완료 Passive voice: Present Simple & Present Perfect
수동태 = be동사 + 과거분사

→ be동사(단순현재형) + 과거분사
Only Robert knows what **is hidden** in his confidential documents.
Robert만이 기밀 문서에 무엇이 숨겨져 있는지 알고 있습니다.

The bodies **are found** by the police.   시체는 경찰에 의해 발견됩니다.

→ be동사(현재완료형) + 과거분사
Many graves **have been dug** here.   많은 무덤이 이곳에 파였습니다.

Alfie **has been hit** by David.   Alfie는 David에게 맞았습니다.

→ 행위에 초점이 맞춰져 있고, 행위의 주체는 알려져 있지 않거나 중요하지 않을 때
Jessica's B&B **is booked**. There are no rooms available.
Jessica의 B&B는 예약이 찼습니다. 구할 수 있는 방이 없습니다.

The stone circles **are** often **described** in archeology books.
스톤 서클은 고고학 서적에서 자주 묘사됩니다.

You can go to your room now, Olive. It **has been cleaned**.
이제 객실로 가도 돼요, Olive. 객실이 청소되었어요.

My car **has been stolen**. I need a new one.   제 차는 도난당했어요. 새 차가 필요해요.

→ 행위의 주체가 알려져 있거나 중요할 때 → 수동태 + *by* + 행위자
Olive **is served by** an unfriendly shop assistant.   Olive는 불친절한 매장 직원에게 응대를 받습니다.

Olive **is introduced** to Beatrice **by** Curtis.   Olive는 Curtis에 의해 Beatrice에게 소개됩니다.

The theft **hasn't been reported by** Robert.   절도 사건은 Robert에 의해 신고되지 않았습니다.

The confidential documents **haven't been read by** Olive's boss yet.
기밀 문서는 아직 Olive의 보스에 의해 읽히지 않았습니다.

## 수동태로 변형하기 Passive voice: Transformations

Somebody **has reported** the fight to the police.

→ The fight **has been reported** to the police.
  누군가가 싸움을 경찰에 신고했습니다. → 싸움이 경찰에 신고되었습니다.
  (*somebody* = 행위의 주체를 알 수 없으며 중요하지도 않으므로, '*by* + 행위자'를 덧붙이지 않음)

People **describe** the stone circles in books.

→ The stone circles **are described** in books.
  사람들은 책에서 스톤 서클을 묘사합니다. → 스톤 서클은 책에서 묘사됩니다.
  (*people* = 행위의 주체를 알 수 없으며 중요하지도 않으므로, '*by* + 행위자'를 덧붙이지 않음)

Wild animals **find** the bodies. → The bodies **are found by** wild animals.
  야생동물들은 시체를 발견합니다. → 시체는 야생동물들에 의해 발견됩니다.

Curtis **has invited** Olive to a party. → Olive **has been invited** to a party **by** Curtis.
  Curtis는 Olive를 파티에 초대했습니다. → Olive는 Curtis에 의해 파티에 초대되었습니다.

# Communication situations

**Read the following dialogues between a pollster and a passer-by. Check the list of words and phrases below.**

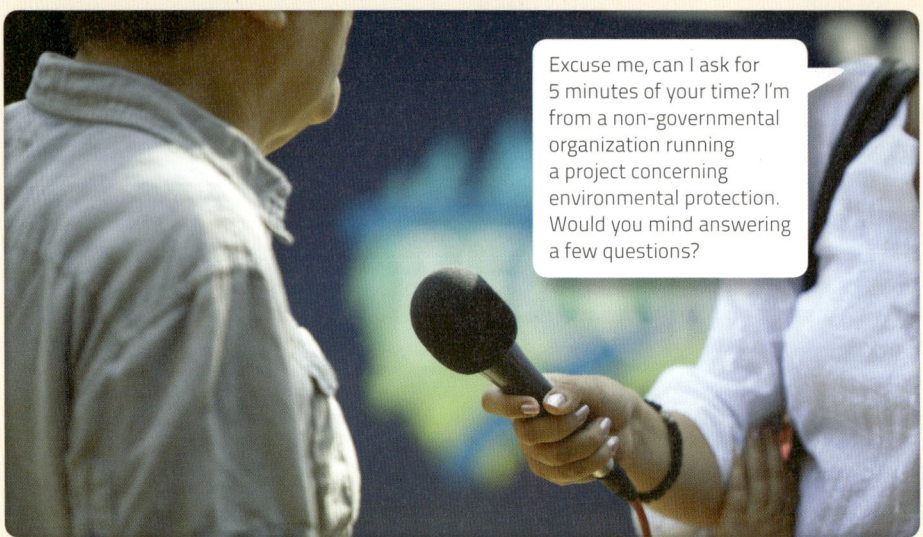

> Excuse me, can I ask for 5 minutes of your time? I'm from a non-governmental organization running a project concerning environmental protection. Would you mind answering a few questions?

### Dialogue 1

**Passer-by:** Sure. I'm an eco-freak myself so I'll be happy to answer your questions.

**Pollster:** Lovely. OK, the first question is: how can our planet be protected?

**Passer-by:** Well, there is a number of small things that can be done.

**Pollster:** Such as?

**Passer-by:** Let's start with water that can be saved.

**Pollster:** And the classic example here would be: turn off the water tap while shaving.

**Passer-by:** Or take a shower instead of a bath.

**Pollster:** True, it can be done, painful as it would be.

**Passer-by:** Or gather rainwater to use it again for a different purpose.

**Pollster:** Right, it would require some additional work but it can be done, certainly.

**Passer-by:** So, would that be all?

**Pollster:** Yes. Thank you for your time!

**non-governmental** 비정부의, 민간의 | **environmental protection** 환경 보호 | **eco-freak** 열렬한 환경 보호론자 | **turn off** ~을 잠그다, 끄다 | **tap** 수도꼭지

### Dialogue 2

**Passer-by:** All right, but just a few questions, please.

**Pollster:** Of course, as promised. Do you know in what ways our planet and its whole ecosystem are being destroyed?

**Passer-by:** Yes, of course I do.

**Pollster:** Could you give any examples?

**Passer-by:** Rainforests are cut down.

**Pollster:** And what are the consequences?

**Passer-by:** The wildlife is endangered.

**Pollster:** Yes, that's really sad.

**Passer-by:** So, would that be all?

**Pollster:** Yes. Thank you for your time!

**wildlife** 야생동물

### Dialogue 3

**Passer-by:** I appreciate what you do but right now I'm in a hurry. Sorry.

**Pollster:** OK. No problem. Have a nice day.

### Dialogue 4

**Passer-by:** Sure. I'm an eco-freak myself so I'll be happy to answer your questions.

**Pollster:** Lovely. OK, the first question is: how can our planet be protected?

**Passer-by:** First of all, renewable resources should be taken into consideration.

**Pollster:** Yes? Keep talking, please.

**Passer-by:** For example, a solar power plant in which energy is generated from the sun.

**Pollster:** We couldn't agree more.

**Passer-by:** And solar power plants are built relatively cheaply, compared to others.

**Pollster:** Yeah, you're probably right.

**Passer-by:** So, would that be all?

**Pollster:** Yes. Thank you for your time!

**renewable** 재생 가능한 | **take into consideration** 고려하다, 참작하다 | **power plant** 발전소 | **relatively** 비교적, 상대적으로

# Vocabulary plus

**affect** 영향을 미치다

**alien** 외계인

**based on** ~에 기반한

**become extinct** 멸종하다

**bin** 쓰레기통

**carbon dioxide** 이산화탄소

**cause** 원인, 이유

**coal mine** 탄광

**complex** 복잡한

**consist of** ~으로 구성되다, 이루어지다

**eco-friendly** 친환경적인

**endangered species** 멸종위기종

**exaggeration** 과장

**exploit** 착취하다, 이용하다

**fossil fuels** 화석 연료

**foundation** 기초, 기반, 토대

**global warming** 지구 온난화

**greed** 탐욕, 욕심

**greenhouse effect** 온실 효과

**hazardous** 위험한

**imbalance** 불균형

**invade** 침략하다, 쳐들어오다

**lack** 부족, 결핍

**leave something on** ~을 켜 놓다

**polluted** 오염된, 더럽혀진

**pressure** 압박, 압력

**rare** 희귀한, 드문

**statement** 진술, 성명

**switch off** ~을 끄다

**waste** 폐기물, 쓰레기

**wind** 바람

# Cultural tips

## Did you know that ...?

The imperial units, or the imperial system, is a collection of measurement units used in the UK. Have a look at some examples below, as compared to the metric system of measurement:

1 inch = 0.0254 metre
1 foot = 0.3048 metre
1 mile = 1,609.344 metres
1 ounce = 0.028 litre
1 pint = 0.568 litre

The imperial system is very similar to the American system but there are some differences.

# Scene 10 (22)  Film dialogue and vocabulary

**Read the dialogue between Alfie (A), Cloutier (C) and Olive (O).
Check the list of words and phrases below.**

You know, shooting a man for the first time is like doing a parachute jump. After the first time you hardly give it a thought!

How many men have you killed, exactly?

A: That's a big question! ... Most of them I killed when I was in the Armed Forces. The famous Special Air Service ... We were the best! I loved that job!

C: Did you hear that?

O: Alfie, give him the gun!

| Vocabulary | | | | |
|---|---|---|---|---|
| | do a parachute jump | 낙하산 점프를 하다 | question | 질문 |
| | hardly | 조금도 ~않다, 거의 ~하지 않다 | Armed Forces | 군대 |
| | give a thought | 생각하다 | Special Air Service | (영국의) 공수특전단 |
| | exactly | 정확히 | love | 대단히 좋아하다 |

**level A2**

## What should Olive do?

negotiate     shoot at Alfie
◎ A2-10-02     ◎ A2-10-03

**O:** Alfie, we can do better than this! Let's just put down the guns and go back to London. The money Cloutier's promised you … It's yours!

**A:** Sounds like a plan! But this one here … is staying in the forest.

**A:** Are you out of your mind? You shot at me? I'm your bloody best friend! (…) David, wow! That was as good as mine! … But I want you to know this – I behaved badly towards you, that's true! But it's only because Olive clearly likes you better than me! So, no hard feelings, yeah?

**D:** None whatsoever!

**A:** Really? … Oh shit!

**Game over.**
Try again.

| | | |
|---|---|---|
| sound like | ~처럼 들리다 | |
| forest | 숲 | |

**Vocabulary**

| | | |
|---|---|---|
| behave | 행동하다, 처신하다 | |
| badly | 못되게, 불친절하게 | |
| true | 맞는, 사실인 | |
| Shit! | 젠장! | |

level A2  Scene 10 (22)

# Grammar explanations

## 형용사의 최상급 Superlative of adjectives

→ 1음절 → the + -est
  old → older → the oldest
  small → smaller → the smallest

→ 2음절 + -y → the + -iest
  funny → funnier → the funniest
  pretty → prettier → the prettiest

→ 자음 + 모음 + 자음 → the + 이중자음 + -est
  hot → hotter → the hottest
  big → bigger → the biggest
  sad → sadder → the saddest

→ 3음절 이상 → the most + 형용사
  expensive → more expensive → the most expensive
  important → more important → the most important

**Remember!**

good → best:
She's the best thief I know.

bad → worst:
It was the worst day of my life.

## 부사 Adverbs

부사는 동작을 묘사하며, *how, when, where, how much* 같은 의문문에 답한다.
형용사는 다음과 같이 부사로 만들 수 있다:

### 규칙 변화

**+ ly**
important → importantly / deep → deeply / quiet → quietly / general → generally

**-y → -ily**
easy → easily / heavy → heavily / happy → happily / angry → angrily

**-le → -ly**
comfortable → comfortably / possible → possibly / respectable → respectably / sociable → sociably

**-ic → + -ally**
basic → basically / scientific → scientifically / historic → historically / linguistic → linguistically

### 불규칙 변화

good → **well**   fast → **fast**   late → **late**
bad → **badly**   hard → **hard**

-ly를 붙여 부사를 만드는 경우, 의미가 변하는 형용사들:
hard 힘든, 어려운 → **hardly** 전혀 ~않다, 거의 ~않다
I **hardly** know you.  저는 당신을 전혀 몰라요.

near 가까운 → **nearly** 하마터면, 거의
I **nearly** believed you.  하마터면 당신을 믿을 뻔했어요.

late 늦은 → **lately** 요즈음, 최근에
I've been very busy **lately**.  저는 요즘 아주 바빠요.

## 부사의 비교급 Comparative of adverbs
부사의 비교급 = 형용사의 비교급

**-er / -ier**
fast → fast**er** / late → lat**er** / early → earl**ier**

**more + ...**
carefully → **more** carefully / perfectly → **more** perfectly / stupidly → **more** stupidly

> **Remember!**
> well → **better**:
> Olive works **better** than Cloutier.
>
> badly → **worse**:
> David fights **worse** than Alfie.

## 동작을 비교하는 *than*

**A** than B     A speaks more loudly **than** B.

## 부사의 최상급 Superlative of adverbs
부사의 최상급 = 형용사의 최상급

**the -est / -iest**
fast → the fast**est** / late → the lat**est** / early → the earl**iest**

**most + ...**
carefully → **most** carefully / perfectly → **most** perfectly / stupidly → **most** stupidly

> **Remember!**
> well → **best**:
> She likes you the **best**.
>
> badly → **worst**:
> They behaved in the **worst** possible way.

# Communication situations

**Read the following dialogues between a publisher and a journalist.**

As this is going to be your very first independent article written for us, we need to discuss it properly. You know that I'd like it to be dynamic and dangerous, something to really get the adrenalin flowing. So what are you going to write about?

### Dialogue 1

**Journalist:** I appreciate your trust. The article will be about a stuntman.

**Publisher:** A stuntman? How original. But what are you going to say about him?

**Journalist:** I'm going to compare his job with other risky jobs.

**Publisher:** Any examples?

**Journalist:** Being a stuntman results in as many injuries as being a firefighter.

**Publisher:** What? You must be joking!

**Journalist:** Consider all the skin burns.

**Publisher:** I see … But is that all they have in common?

**Journalist:** Well, I wonder who inhales more smoke on the job.

**Publisher:** I think a firefighter will win this contest every time. That's not enough for an article, though.

**Journalist:** How about "The Fainting Firemen" for a header?

**Publisher:** Excuse me? Do you mean the loss of consciousness among firefighters? Hmm. Can you back it up with any statistics?

**Journalist:** Yes, I have quite a lot of data already.

**Publisher:** Hmm. OK, why not. Prepare the first draft for tomorrow and we'll see.

**get the adrenalin flowing** 아드레날린을 분비시키다, 몹시 흥분시키다 | **stuntman** 스턴트맨 | **firefighter** 소방관 | **burn** 화상, 덴 자국 | **have in common** 공통점이 있다 | **inhale** 들이마시다 | **contest** 대결, 경연 | **fainting** 실신하는, 졸도하는 | **loss of consciousness** 의식 불명 | **back up** 뒷받침하다, 지지하다 | **first draft** 초고

### Dialogue 2

**Journalist:** Yes, finally! My big chance! I'm going to write about a firefighter.

**Publisher:** A firefighter? That's how you are going to attract the reader? It's just an ordinary profession these days.

**Journalist:** Well, it all depends on how you present it.

**Publisher:** Now it's getting interesting. Go on.

**Journalist:** You might say that firefighters are more respected than police officers.

**Publisher:** I think that's going too far.

**Journalist:** Or that they must always stay cool, just like paramedics.

**Publisher:** Hmm, maybe that is a good way to talk about risky professions. Let's give it a try.

**stay cool** 침착함을 유지하다 | **paramedic** 긴급 의료원, 의료 보조원

### Dialogue 3

**Journalist:** All right! How about a ranking of the most dangerous professions?

**Publisher:** Hmm. I'm not sure about that. Who are you going to include so that it's not just another "top-ten" chart?

**Journalist:** I'll start with a commando.

**Publisher:** Oh, that's a great idea! What are you going to write about him?

**Journalist:** Or her!

**Publisher:** Come on! Have you ever seen a female commando?

**Journalist:** No, but I'm going to look for one.

**Publisher:** I bet you won't find any. Women are physically weaker and more sensitive than men. They usually choose less aggressive jobs.

**Journalist:** Those are just stereotypes!

**Publisher:** Really? Then prove me wrong!

**Journalist:** You bet I will.

**Publisher:** OK. I look forward to the conversation!

**chart** 차트, 표 | **commando** 특공대원, 의용군 | **prove somebody wrong** ~가 틀렸음을 입증하다

# Vocabulary plus

**as stupid as a donkey** 당나귀처럼 미련한

**bone** 뼈

**bruise** 멍, 타박상

**catchy** 재미있고 기억하기 쉬운

**concussion** 뇌진탕

**damage** 손상, 피해

**fatal** 치명적인, 죽음을 초래하는

**get carried away** (자제력을 잃을 정도로) 흥분하다

**have one's heart set on** ~을 갈망하다

**hot-headed** 성마른, 성질이 급한

**impairment** 손상; 장애

**interview** 인터뷰, 회견

**interviewee** 인터뷰 대상자

**journal** 정기 간행물, 잡지, 신문

**Let's keep it this way.** 이대로 두자.

**Let's see where it takes us.** 어떻게 될지 보자.

**nurse** 간호사

**occupational hazard** 직업상 위험

**routine** 일과

**spine** 척추, 등뼈

**stunt** 아슬아슬한 연기

**thesis** 명제, 논제

**to say the least** 최대한 완곡하게 말해서

**unique** 독특한

**vital organs** (심장 등 생명 유지에 필요한) 중요 기관

# Cultural tips

## Did you know that ...?

The SAS or Special Air Service, is a Special Operations Organisation of the British Army. It was founded in 1941. The SAS is known to be a very secret organisation. Its members often do not tell anyone except close family that they are in it.

# Scene 11 (23) — Film dialogue and vocabulary

**Read the dialogue between Olive (O), David (D), Alfie (A) and Cloutier (C). Check the list of words and phrases below.**

> Good! OK, guys, that looks pretty solid, doesn't it?

**O:** Now, we need to organise some food and stuff for you. We can't let you starve or freeze to death here, can we? Now, about the money …

**D:** There is still 50k in Cloutier's car! I can go and …

**A:** There is no money in your car, is there?

**C:** What? Business has been slow recently! I really wanted to pay you! … A thousand pounds or so!

**A:** 1,000 quid? You're joking, right? … But on the other hand, a grand is not actually bad for a four hours' work, is it?

**O:** I'm losing the little respect I had for you, Alfie. Now, where did you put my wallet?

**A:** It's in my shop, in London. Together with his!

| Vocabulary | | | |
|---|---|---|---|
| solid | 튼튼한, 견고한 | joke (about) | (~에 대해) 장난하다, 농담하다 |
| organize | 마련하다, 준비하다 | on the other hand | 한편으로는 |
| starve | 굶주리다 | actually | 사실, 실제로 |
| freeze to death | 얼어 죽다 | hour | 1시간 |
| Business is slow. | 장사가 잘 안 되다, 사업이 부진하다 | respect | 존중, 존경 |
| | | wallet | 지갑 |
| recently | 요즘, 최근에 | | |

# level A2

**Read David's monologue. Check the list of words and phrases below.**

Sleeping bag, compact, water-proof, 35 pounds! No way!…

**D:** Space blanket, keeps you warm in all weathers, 6 pounds! All right!… A bucket! 1 pound 50. Will one be enough? Damn it!… Toilet paper – regular or extra soft? Regular is only 99 p! Sorry guys! (…) I need some sandwiches! But I can't really afford them, so …

### Vocabulary

| | |
|---|---|
| sleeping bag | 침낭 |
| compact | 아주 작은, 소형의 |
| water-proof | 방수의 |
| space blanket | 비상 (은박) 담요 |
| keep warm | 따뜻하게 해 주다 |
| in all weathers | 어떤 날씨에도 |
| toilet paper | (보통 두루마리로 된) 휴지 |
| regular | 일반적인, 표준의 |
| afford | (금전적) 형편이 되다 |

## What should David do?

haggle — A2-11-03

beg — A2-11-04

**D:** I noticed they're quite stale. Actually, their expiry date is today! Can you give me a discount? I could pay you … 50 p for each?

**S:** No problem, mate!

**D:** Please! I need to feed my friends. If I don't bring them any food …

**S:** You can have all the sandwiches free of charge. They are stale and I need to get rid of them anyway. Yeah, take them all! And good luck.

| Vocabulary | | |
|---|---|---|
| notice | 알아채다 |
| stale | (만든 지) 오래된, 신선하지 않은 |
| expiry date | 유통 기한 |
| discount (on) | (~에 대한) 할인 |
| feed | 먹이다 |
| bring | 가져다주다 |
| free of charge | 공짜로 |
| stale | (만든 지) 오래된, 신선하지 않은 |
| get rid of | 처분하다, 없애다 |

# Grammar explanations

## 부가의문문 Question tags

+

긍정문 ➡ 부정 부가의문문

It is a lovely day today, **isn't it?**  오늘 날씨가 참 좋네요, 그렇지 않나요?

I am the best, **aren't I?**  제가 최고입니다, 그렇지 않나요?

He will join us in the evening, **won't he?**  그는 저녁 때 우리와 함께할 거예요, 그렇지 않나요?

We have already seen this film twice, **haven't we?**
우리는 이미 이 영화를 두 번이나 보았어요, 그렇지 않나요?

I called you yesterday, **didn't I?**  저는 어제 당신에게 전화했어요, 그렇지 않나요?

There is this famous music festival in your town, **isn't there?**
당신의 마을에서는 이 유명한 뮤직 페스티벌이 열려요, 그렇지 않나요?

You can pick Tom up from the airport, **can't you?**  Tom을 공항에서 태워올 수 있죠, 그렇지 않나요?

You could do me favour, **couldn't you?**  제 부탁을 들어주실 수 있죠, 그렇지 않나요?

Jerry would always be the first in running, **wouldn't he?**
Jerry는 달리기에서 항상 일등일 거예요, 그렇지 않나요?

They should be home by now, **shouldn't they?**  그들은 지금쯤 집에 있을 거예요, 그렇지 않나요?

부정문 ➡ 긍정 부가의문문

Beatrice doesn't like Olive very much, **does she?** Beatrice는 Olive를 별로 좋아하지 않아요, 그렇죠?

She won't be happy to host Olive again, **will she?** 그녀는 Olive를 다시 접대하고 싶지 않을 거예요, 그렇죠?

You haven't gone to the shop yet, **have you?** 당신은 아직 매장에 가지 않았어요, 그렇죠?

Olive, you didn't buy the dress only for the party, **did you?**
Olive, 파티를 위해서만 드레스를 산 것은 아니군요, 그렇죠?

There wasn't anybody at home, **was there?** 집에는 아무도 없었어요, 그렇죠?

He can't cook very well, **can he?** 그는 요리를 별로 잘하지 않아요, 그렇죠?

We couldn't refresh the painting at any time, **could we?**
우리는 언제라도 그림을 새것처럼 보이게 할 수 있어요, 그렇죠?

She wouldn't call the police, **would she?** 그녀는 경찰에게 전화하지 않을 거예요, 그렇죠?

You are not in good health yet. You shouldn't do such exercises, **should you?**
당신은 아직 건강이 좋지 못해요. 그런 운동은 하면 안 돼요, 그렇죠?

## 의문대명사 Interrogative pronouns

**who** (사람)
Who is there? 거기 누구십니까?

**when** (시간)
When did you call her? Yesterday or two days ago?
언제 그녀에게 전화했나요? 어제였나요, 아니면 이틀 전이었나요?

**where** (장소)
Where is my money? Is it in your car, Cloutier?
제 돈은 어디에 있나요? 당신의 차 안에 있나요, Cloutier?

**why** (이유)
Why did you accept Cloutier's proposal? You know he's a liar, don't you?
왜 Cloutier의 제안을 받아들인 거야? 그가 거짓말쟁이라는 것을 알잖아, 그렇지 않니?

**which** (사물, 제한된 선택의 여지)
Which sandwich do you want, with ham or cheese?
어떤 샌드위치를 원하세요, 햄이 든 것, 아니면 치즈가 든 것?

**what** (사물, 넓은 선택의 여지)
What do you want from me, Cloutier?
저한테 무엇을 원하나요, Cloutier?

**how many** (수, 셀 수 있는 명사)
How many cases have you solved, David?
사건을 몇 건이나 해결했나요, David?

**how much** (양, 셀 수 없는 명사)
How much money do we need?
우리에게 돈이 얼마나 필요한가요?

**how long** (기간)
How long have you been here?
당신은 이곳에 얼마나 있었나요?

**how often** (빈도)
How often do you steal paintings, Olive?
얼마나 자주 그림을 훔치나요, Olive?

# Communication situations

**Read the following dialogues between a shop assistant and a client in a supermarket and grocer's shop.**

Good morning, how can I help you?

## Dialogue 1

**Client:** Good morning. I know it's a supermarket but I'm lost.

**Shop assistant:** Don't worry. I'll assist you along the aisles. What are you looking for?

**Client:** Let me see. Snacks are first on my list.

**Shop assistant:** Yeah, a snack is always a good start. So, where exactly shall we go?

**Client:** Let's go to crisps and crackers.

**Shop assistant:** Just so you know, you've chosen the longest aisle. The crisps are on your left and the crackers are on your right.

**Client:** And things like pistachios and almonds?

**Shop assistant:** Healthy foods, right. They are over there. You have to put them in a bag and weigh them yourself.

**Client:** OK. No problem. I'll go and get some. Thanks for your help.

**Shop assistant:** No problem. Have a nice day!

---

**aisle** 통로, 복도 | **crisps** (얇게 잘라 튀긴) 칩 | **weigh** 무게를 달다

### Dialogue 2

**Client:** I'd like some dairy products. Can I get them here?

**Shop assistant:** Sorry, we are a convenience store. We've just got the basic products. And actually no dairies at all.

**Client:** I see. I'll just take a coke, please.

**Shop assistant:** A bottle or a can?

**Client:** A bottle. And I'd like it cold, please.

**Shop assistant:** Sure. Anything else?

**Client:** Maybe a packet of cigarettes, please.

**Shop assistant:** Sorry, you are under 18. You are not allowed to buy cigarettes.

**dairy products** 유제품 | **convenience store** 편의점 | **cigarette** 담배

### Dialogue 3

**Client:** Are you still open?

**Shop assistant:** Yes, we are. What can I get you?

**Client:** Oh, I've got the whole shopping list here. Let's start with dairy.

**Shop assistant:** Sure.

**Client:** 5 eggs, a packet of cheese and two tubs of cottage cheese, please.

**Shop assistant:** Here you are. Would you like anything else?

**Client:** Yes. I'll take two rolls, two doughnuts and a croissant, please.

**Shop assistant:** Will that be all?

**Client:** And a box of cornflakes. That's all.

**Shop assistant:** Here you are. That will be £15.65.

**cottage cheese** 코티지 치즈 | **roll** 롤빵, 둥근 빵

# Vocabulary plus

**a jar of jam** 잼 한 병

**a loaf of bread** 빵 한 덩어리

**a pack of butter** 버터 한 팩

**basket** 바구니, 바스켓

**beverage** 음료

**bubbles** 거품

**caffeine-free** 카페인이 없는

**cash register** 금전 등록기

**chewing gum** 껌

**cleaner** 세정제

**condiment** 조미료, 양념

**container** 그릇, 용기

**expire** (기한이) 만료되다

**expiry date** 유통 기한

**fizzy** 거품이 나는, 발포성의

**flavor** 맛, 풍미

**good at** ~을 잘하는

**grocery section** 식료품 코너

**hot sauce** 핫 소스

**I have never heard of such a thing.** 그런 건 한 번도 들어본 적 없어요.

**in case (that)** ~할 경우에 대비해서

**It doesn't agree with me.** 그건 내 체질에 안 받아요.

**manage by oneself** 혼자 힘으로 살아나가다

**milk** 우유

**nuts** 견과

**packaged** 포장된

**pasta** 파스타

**salt and pepper** 소금과 후추

**Sorry for bothering you.** 귀찮게 해서 미안해요.

**tub of yogurt** 요구르트 한 통

**under the influence of** ~에 취해

# Cultural tips

## Did you know that ...?

The pound is subdivided into 100 pence. The singular form is "penny". The penny's symbol is "p". While shopping, people often use this abbreviation instead of giving the full word after a certain amount of pence, for example: 50p /fıftı pi:/.

# Scene 12 (24) — Film dialogue and vocabulary

**Read the dialogue between David (D) and Olive (O).
Check the list of words and phrases below.**

I can't believe you still had 20 pounds and you never said a word about it!

**D:** Those poor chaps! ... We left them with stale sandwiches!

**O:** The money wasn't mine! I found it in Marco's pocket, but I decided that after all the things that have happened to you because of me at least I owe you a decent meal.

**D:** I still need to ask you to give back the documents to Murray ... who is pretty mad at you! ... You could stop this! He's not like Bill from the pub whom you can beat up when he bothers you. He's got lots of information about you and the resources to turn your life into a nightmare. So, please, end this!

**O:** When you're in my line of work, there's always someone powerful who wants you dead. This is what happens when you steal from rich people. I can't end this! ... Not yet! But this could end for you, Constable Owen! Just go back to Old Berry and return to your old life!

**D:** My old life ... You ruined it! There's no returning to anything. I'm stuck with you.

**O:** I'm quite pleased you are!

level **A2**

| Vocabulary | | | |
|---|---|---|---|
| chap | 녀석, 놈, 친구 | nightmare | 악몽 |
| pocket | 주머니 | end | 끝내다 |
| decide | 결심하다 | line of work | 계통의 일, 분야의 일 |
| owe | 빚지고 있다 | always | 늘, 항상 |
| decent | 제대로 된, 괜찮은 | powerful | 권력 있는 |
| meal | 밥, 식사 | dead | 죽은 |
| be mad (at) | (~에게) 몹시 화나다 | return | 되돌아가다 |
| pretty | 아주, 매우 | ruin | 망치다 |
| beat up | ~를 두들겨 패다 | be stuck with | ~을 떨쳐 버리지 못하다 |
| bother | 귀찮게 하다, 괴롭히다 | pleased | 좋은, 기쁜 |
| resources | 자력, 재원, 자산 | | |

**Olive gets out of the car for a moment. David's phone rings.
What should David do?**

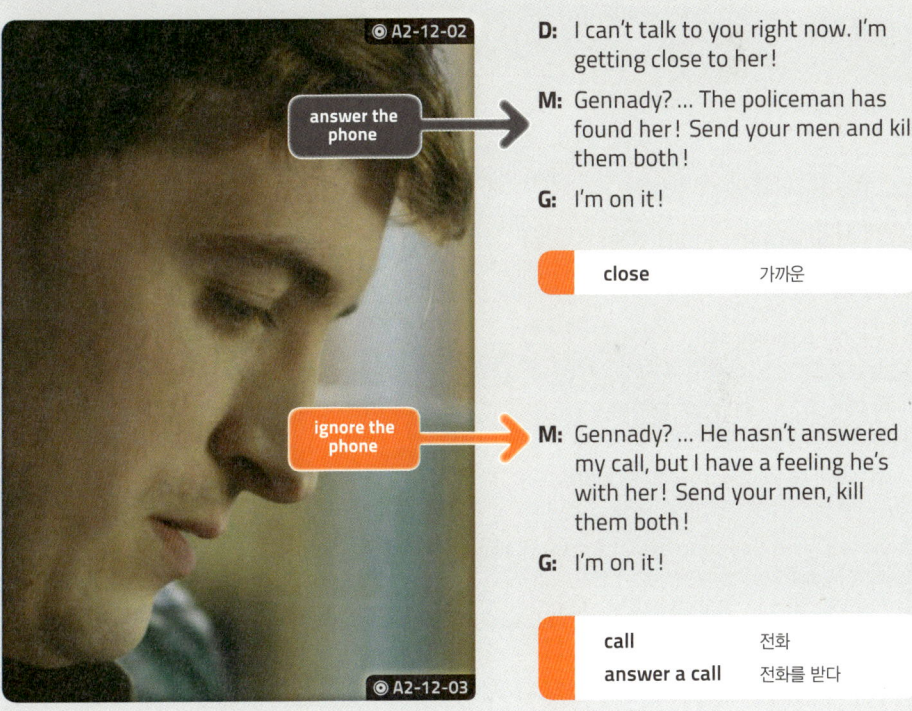

A2-12-02

answer the phone

D: I can't talk to you right now. I'm getting close to her!

M: Gennady?... The policeman has found her! Send your men and kill them both!

G: I'm on it!

| close | 가까운 |
|---|---|

ignore the phone

M: Gennady?... He hasn't answered my call, but I have a feeling he's with her! Send your men, kill them both!

G: I'm on it!

A2-12-03

| call | 전화 |
|---|---|
| answer a call | 전화를 받다 |

level A2  Scene 12 (24)

# Grammar explanations

## 조건문 Zero conditional

> if + 단순현재, 단순현재

➜ 사실:
 If you **heat** water, it **boils**.　물을 가열하면, 끓습니다.
 If you **exercise** regularly, you **feel** better.　규칙적으로 운동하면, 기분이 좋아집니다.
 If you **freeze** water, it **turns** into ice.　물을 얼리면, 얼음으로 변합니다.

➜ 진실:
 If I **don't know** the answer, I **get** upset easily.　답을 모르면, 나는 쉽게 속상해집니다.
 If you **press** this button, the light **comes** on.　이 버튼을 누르면, 불이 들어옵니다.
 If you **are** out of petrol, your car **stops**.　기름이 떨어지면, 차가 섭니다.

> 조건문에서 콤마의 유무에 유의한다:
> if + 단순현재 + , + 단순현재 (콤마 있음)
> cf. 단순현재 + if + 단순현재 (콤마 없음)

## 시간부사절: when　Time clause: when

> when + 단순현재

I will call you **when** I **get** home.
집에 도착하면 당신에게 전화할게요.

I can't talk to you **when** I**'m** at work.
일하고 있을 때는 당신과 이야기할 수 없어요.

David will give the shop assistant more money **when** he **comes** back again.
David가 다시 돌아오면 그는 매장 직원에게 돈을 더 줄 것입니다.

Gennady's people will hurt Olive and David **when** they **see** them.
Gennady의 부하들은 Olive와 David를 만나면 그들을 해칠 것입니다.

Let me know **when** we **can talk** without witnesses.
목격자 없이 이야기할 수 있을 때 알려 주세요.

## 복문 Complex sentences
= 주절 + 종속절

**David talked to Robert** who asked him about Olive.
David는 Olive에 관해 물어 본 Robert와 이야기했습니다.

**He is not like Bill from the pub** whom you can beat up.
그는 당신이 때려눕힐 수 있는, 술집의 Bill 같은 사람이 아닙니다.

**Olive has got the documents** that Robert wants.
Olive는 Robert가 원하는 문서를 가지고 있습니다.

**Olive came back to the car** which was parked in the backyard.
Olive는 뒷마당에 주차된 차로 돌아갔습니다.

**This is what happens** when you steal from rich people.
이것이 부자를 털 때 발생하는 일입니다.

**Old Berry is the place** where everything started.
Old Berry는 모든 일이 시작된 곳입니다.


**who** (사람, 행위의 주체):
**who** asked him about Olive.   Olive에 관해 물어 본 사람 = Robert

**whom** (사람, 행위의 대상):
**whom** you can beat up.   당신이 때려눕힐 수 있는 사람 = Bill

**that** (사물):
**that** Robert wants.   Robert가 원하는 것 = 문서

**which** (사물):
**which** was parked in the backyard.   뒷마당에 주차된 것 = 차

**when** (시간):
**when** you steal from rich people.   부자를 털 때

**where** (장소):
**where** everything started.   모든 일이 시작된 곳 = Old Berry

level A2  Scene 12 (24)

# Communication situations

**Read the following dialogues between a grandfather and his grandchild discussing computers and technology.**

My dear, I'm so glad you could come. I've had this thing for a week already but I don't know where to start. How do I use it?

## Dialogue 1

**Grandchild:** Hi grandpa! Show me what you've got there.

**Grandpa:** This nice and shiny black laptop!

**Grandchild:** It looks great. Let's see what operating system you've got.

**Grandpa:** And ...?

**Grandchild:** I know this system, so no problem. What do you need it for, anyway?

**Grandpa:** I need a computer for writing. I want to write the history of our family.

**Grandchild:** What a lovely idea!

**Grandpa:** Yes, I think so too.

**Grandchild:** OK. Click on this icon and look at the toolbar.

**Grandpa:** What's a toolbar? Oh, I see. What are these signs for?

**Grandchild:** Why don't you try them out? That's the best way to learn.

**Grandpa:** Will you stay with me in case I mess something up?

**Grandchild:** You'll be fine! Just remember to click on the disc icon to save it.

**Grandpa:** Oh yes, good idea! Thanks, my dear.

grandpa 할아버지 | shiny 반짝거리는, 빛나는 | operating system 운영 체제 | toolbar 툴바 | save 저장하다

## Dialogue 2

**Grandchild:** Hi grandpa. Don't worry, I'll teach you. What have you got there?

**Grandpa:** I knew I could count on you! Here, it's my new smart phone. Unfortunately, it's completely black.

**Grandchild:** You have to turn it on. Here's the button.

**Grandpa:** Hey, it worked! So, is it ready to make phone calls?

**Grandchild:** You have to enter your PIN first.

**Grandpa:** What is it?

**Grandchild:** A sequence of digits to unblock your phone.

**Grandpa:** Oh yes, they mentioned it at the shop. Here it is. Can I call now?

**Grandchild:** Well, why don't you give it a try?

**Grandpa:** Great! I'm calling your granny. She'll be very surprised!

make a (phone) call 전화를 걸다 | enter 입력하다 | sequence of digits 연속적인 숫자 | granny 할머니

## Dialogue 3

**Grandpa:** And what do you think?

**Grandchild:** Oh, it's a very good machine, grandpa.

**Grandpa:** Is it really? How do you know?

**Grandchild:** I can see it has a very fast hard drive and a multi-core processor.

**Grandpa:** I don't understand a thing but I trust you know what you're talking about, my dear.

hard drive 하드 드라이브 | multi-core processor 멀티 코어 프로세서 | I don't understand a thing. 하나도 못 알아듣겠구나.

# Vocabulary plus

**although** ~이긴 하지만

**as good as any** 그저 그런

**birth year** 출생연도

**cordless** 무선의

**cover** 커버, 덮개

**crack** (암호 등을) 풀다

**dictionary** 사전

**display** (컴퓨터) 디스플레이

**envelope** 봉투

**explore** 탐험하다, 답사하다

**for later** 나중을 위해

**graphics card** 그래픽 카드

**hardware** 하드웨어

**headphones** 헤드폰

**Here I come!** 내가 간다!

**hole** 구멍

**impossible** 불가능한

**Internet connection** 인터넷 연결

**keyboard** 키보드

**keypad** 키패드

**No worries.** 걱정하지 마세요. / 괜찮아요.

**on one's own** 혼자서, 단독으로

**port** 포트(컴퓨터의 주변 기기 접속 단자)

**printer** 프린터

**provider** 서비스 제공 업체

**recipient** 받는 사람, 수신자

**say something out loud** 소리 내어 말하다

**scissors** 가위

**security settings** 보안 설정

**send a message** 메시지를 보내다

**sheet** (종이) 한 장

**socket** (플러그 등을) 꽂는 곳

**specifications** 사양

**starter pack**
스타터 팩(게임 등에서 시작하는 사람을 위한 패키지)

**take ages** (시간이) 한참 걸리다

**text** 문자를 보내다

**There's method in this madness.**
미친 짓처럼 보여도 나름대로 생각이 있겠지.

**type in** 입력하다

# Cultural tips

## Did you know that ...?

Vehicle registration number plates in the UK are rectangular or square in shape. Front plates are white, whereas back plates are yellow. In the U.S., the colours of vehicle registration number plates vary among states.

# Translation 해석

## Scene 1 (13)

### Film dialogue and vocabulary   p. 8~9

A: 저 친구는 좀 어때요, 클로티에?

C: 괜찮아! 마르코는 강하고 튼튼한 젊은이거든. 금방 깰 걸세.

A: 네, 그럴지도요… 그래도 좀 덮어줘야 할 거예요. 저체온증은 고약한 놈이거든요. 정말 자상한 여자예요! 맨손으로 죽여버리고 싶은 이 순간에도 그건 인정할 수밖에 없어요! 마음속은 착하고 친절한 사람이에요!

C: 친절? 그건 아니지! 저 녀석 꼴을 봐!

A: 그건 일 때문이고요. 우릴 안 죽였잖아요, 안 그래요? 담도도 주고 음식에… 양동이까지! 우린 괜찮을 거예요. 이 창고에서 며칠 있다 보면, 우릴 풀어줄 거예요! 휴가나 다름없죠!

C: 정신이 나갔군, 알피! 미쳤어. 그 입 다물지 못하겠나?

A: 못해요. 제가 말하고 사람 사귀는 걸 좋아해서요! 댁도 프랑스인이잖아요. 프랑스인들도 사교적이고 수다스럽지 않아요?

C: 맞는 말이지만 지금은 사교적일 기분이 아니야. 이런 데 갇혀 있잖아. 외딴곳에 곧 죽을 사람이랑 미친 영국놈이랑.

A: 안 죽어요! … 간식 어때요? 뭐 좀 먹죠! 지금쯤 아침 식사 시간일 거예요! 어디 보자… 음, 초코바 세 개 그리고… 햄 샌드위치 그리고 치즈 샌드위치가 있어요.

C: 난 햄 샌드위치로 하지. 평소에 고기로 하루를 시작하거든!

A: 이게… 맛이 좀 이상하네요. 저기… 양동이 좀 주시겠어요?

### Communication situations   p. 12~13

Woman: 오디션 프로그램은 어때, 왜 있잖아, 춤추고, 노래하고, 연기하고… 나는 가끔 보거든.

**Dialogue 1**

Man: 나도야. 나는 음악 오디션 프로그램이라면 다 좋아.

Woman: 아, 그래?

Man: 응. 오디션 프로그램은 성공하기 위한 좋은 방법이라고 생각해.

Woman: 그건 사실이지만… 그런 프로그램에 나오는 사람들은 정직하지 못하고 성공에 기를 쓰는 것 같더라.

Man: 전혀 그렇지 않아. 그 사람들을 너무 엄격하게 판단하고 있구나.

Woman: 그래? 내 생각에, 그런 대회에 참가하는 사람들은 순진한 것 같아.

Man: 전혀 동의하지 않아. 결연한 거지.

Woman: 무슨 뜻이야?

Man: 뭐랄까, 성공을 위해 사는 사람도 있잖아.

Woman: 알아. 그건 전혀 반대하지 않지만, 그래도 내가 봤을 때 오디션 프로그램이 최선의 방법은 아니야.

Man: 그러면 네 생각에 최선의 방법은 뭔데?

Woman: 운과 재능이 중요하지.

Man: 네 말에 일리는 있는지 모르지만, 그래도 재능이 있는 것만으로는 충분하지 않잖아.

Woman: 아, 나도 재능만으로는 충분하지 않다고 생각해. 운도 약간 따라줘야지.

Man: 뭐, 그건 확실하지.

Woman: 그럼 적어도 부분적으로는 우리 의견이 일치하네. 저녁에 대한 시작이 좋은걸.

### Dialogue 2

Man: 뭔지는 알겠는데 그런 프로그램은 안 좋아해.

Woman: 그래? 왜?

Man: 비위에 거슬려.

Woman: 정확히 어떤 점이 거슬리는데?

Man: 뭐랄까, 겉만 번지르르하고, 잘난 체하고, 완벽하게 차려입은 연예인들을 못 견디겠어.

Woman: 심사위원단 말하는 거야?

Man: 맞아. 그 사람들은 잔인하고 무정해.

Woman: 그건 사실이지만 그게 연예계인걸. 무자비한 곳.

Man: 맞는 말이야. 하지만 슬프다, 안 그래?

Woman: 정말 그래. 슬퍼. 이제 더 기분 좋은 주제로 넘어가자. 간식 먹을래?

### Dialogue 3

Man: 뭔지 알겠다. 개인적으로, 나는 오디션 프로그램을 좋아하는 것 같지는 않아.

Woman: 나도 그래. 가끔은 다 너무 한심하게 느껴져.

Man: 내가 맞춰 볼게. 짓궂게 괴롭히는 심사위원단이 싫은 거지?

Woman: 무슨 말인지 모르겠는걸.

Man: 그러니까, 내가 보기에는 그 사람들 아주 불공정하더라고. 그리고 그 사람들도 그냥 연예인일 뿐이잖아, 전문가도 아니고!

Woman: 그래, 그건 사실이지만, 그게 바로 그 프로그램의 의도잖아.

## Scene 2 (14)

### Film dialogue and vocabulary    p. 16~17

M: 데이비드, 올리브랑 있었던 일… 사태가 아주 심각해! 우리 어떻게 하지?

D: 그건 모르겠고, 어제 당신이 날 죽이려던 건 기억나네요!

M: 내가? 오해일세! 내가 올리브 그린에 대해 조사해 봤는데 전문 미술품 절도범일세. 냉정하고 계산적인 여자지…

D: 어젯밤에… 당신 그림을 훔쳤나요?

M: 아니, 더 엄청난 걸 훔쳤어. 사업상 기밀문서를 훔쳐 갔네. 그러니까 그 여자를 찾아서 가져와!

D: 싫어요! 안 해요! 오히려 얘기 끝나는 대로 경찰서에 계신 경사님께 전화해서 모든 걸 신고…

M: 절대 안 돼! 올리브는 나와 내 사업을 망하게 하려는 내 적을 돕고 있어. 자넨 올리브를 도왔고! 자네 상사가 어떻게 할 것 같나? 자넨 실수했어. 하지만 좋은 경찰관이지! 그걸 망치지 말게! 그럼… 날 도울 텐가?

**agree**

D: 제가 올리브를 찾으면… 해쳐서는 안 돼요! 아시겠어요?

M: 당연하지! 사실, 내 밑에서 일해달라고 할 걸세!

D: 좋아요. 할게요!

M: 이걸 쎄! 안전한 전화기일세. 그 여자에 관한 한 특별히 조심해야 해. 올리브의 예전 동료들 이름과 주소야. 거기에서 시작해! 한 가지 더! 슬프지만 자네 어머니가 빚이 있어. 엄청나게 많이! 알고 있었나? 게스트하우스는 내일이라도 내 것이 될 수 있어. 그럼… 더 말할 필요 없겠지?

**refuse**

D: 됐어요!

M: 자네가 안 찾으면… 내 친구들이 찾아! 그러면 곱게 두진 않을 거야! 그건 장담하지!

D: 알았어요! 할게요!

M: 이걸 쎄! 안전한 전화기일세. 그 여자에 관한 한 특별히 조심해야 해. 올리브의 예전 동료들 이름과 주소야. 거기에서 시작해! 한 가지 더! 슬프지만 자네 어머니가 빚이 있어. 엄청나게 많이! 알고 있었나? 게스트하우스는 내일이라도 내 것이 될 수 있어. 그럼… 더 말할 필요 없겠지?

## Communication situations   p. 22~23

**Travel agent:** 안녕하세요. 기다리시게 해서 죄송합니다. 여행사로서는 바쁜 시기, 즉 성수기라서요. 그건 그렇고, 몇 분 정도 저희 카탈로그를 보셨잖아요. 목적지는 정하셨나요?

**Dialogue 1**

**Client:** 아뇨, 못 정했어요. 가 볼 만한 곳을 추천해 주셨으면 좋겠어요.

**Travel agent:** 물론이지요. 그럼 간단한 질문을 하나 드릴게요. 휴가를 활동적으로 보내시고 싶으신가요, 아니면 쉬시면서 경치를 즐기고 싶으신가요?

**Client:** 둘 다 약간씩 있으면 좋을 것 같은데요.

**Travel agent:** 그러시군요. 7일은 관광하고 7일은 해변에서 보내는 패키지 상품을 추천해 드릴게요.

**Client:** 좋아요. 관광 부분에는 어떤 도시들이 포함되어 있나요?

**Travel agent:** 카탈로그를 확인해 볼게요… 스페인의 주요 도시가 언급되어 있네요. 그리고 관광 부분은 마조르카에서 끝납니다.

Client: 페리를 탄다는 뜻이군요.

Travel agent: 네, 바로 그 뜻입니다.

Client: 아 이런, 제가 뱃멀미가 있어서요.

Travel agent: 아, 그거 안타깝네요. 그렇다면 7일 체류 상품을 생각해 보실 수 있겠네요.

Client: 어떤 종류의 호텔에서 묵게 되나요?

Travel agent: 4성급 호텔에서 숙박하시게 될 겁니다.

Client: 객실에 냉방 장치가 있죠?

Travel agent: 네, 그렇습니다.

Client: 좋아요. 싱글룸으로 예약해 주시겠어요?

Travel agent: 바다 전망으로요?

Client: 네, 그러면 좋겠네요.

Travel agent: 알겠습니다. 다 되었습니다. 세부 내용은 모두 이메일로 보내 드릴게요.

### Dialogue 2

Client: 거의 정했어요. 저는 유럽 어딘가에 가고 싶어요.

Travel agent: 알겠습니다. 어떤 종류의 휴가에 관심이 있으신가요, 자가용 휴가, 신혼여행, 아니면 다른 여행?

Client: 자가용 휴가는 뭐죠?

Travel agent: 자기가 직접 마련한 교통수단으로 휴가지까지 가는 휴가예요. 보통 차나 기차가 되죠. 비행기는 전세 내지 않는 이상 너무 비싸니까요. 숙소와 세 끼 식사가 가격에 포함되어 있고요.

Client: 아니에요, 그건 저한테는 안 맞아요.

Travel agent: 아, 그러시군요. 런던에서 주말 휴가를 보내시는 건 어떨까요?

Client: 해외로 나가고 싶어요. 그리고 다음 주 주말에 떠나고 싶어요.

Travel agent: 마드리드를 추천해 드려도 될까요? 아니면 베를린은 어떠세요? 이 도시들은 해외여행으로 2박이나 3박을 하기에 완벽합니다.

Client: 친구들을 데리고 갈 거라서 베를린이 좋은 선택일 것 같아요.

Travel agent: 네, 탁월한 선택입니다. 후회하지 않으실 거예요.

# Scene 3 (15)

### Film dialogue and vocabulary  p. 26~28

J: 유니폼도 안 입었네? 8시 출근이잖아! 지각하겠다!

D: 오늘 휴가 냈어요.

J: 휴가? 어디 아파? 숙취? 단순한 숙취라면… 차와 함께 아침 식사를 하면 나아질 거야. 달걀하고 베이컨으로 해 줄게.

D: 아픈 것도 아니고 숙취도 아니에요. 그냥… 런던에서 중요한 약속이 있어요. 그래서… 엄마 차 좀 빌려야겠어요.

J: 내 차? 네 차는 어쩌고?

**tell the truth**

D: 올리브가 가져갔어요!

J: 네가 빌려줬다는 말이니? 아니면 훔쳐간 거야?

D: 훔쳐갔어요.

D: 알았어요… 어떻게 된 거냐면…

J: 알고 싶지 않아! 정말이야! … 처음엔 둘이 데이트를 하더니 그러다 갑자기 관뒀지! … 그리고 넌 죽상을 하고 다녔어. 난 생각했지. "그래, 그냥 여자야. 이겨낼 거야." 며칠이 지난 지금… 넌 멍한 얼굴로 여기 앉아 있고 차는 없어졌고, 갑자기 일도 뒷전이 된 거야.

D: 그렇게 간단한 게 아니에요! 엄마, 차를 빌려줄 거예요, 말 거예요? 얼른 말해주세요. 20분 뒤에 버스가 떠나니까요!

J: 그래, 알았다! … 그럴 만한 가치가 있는 여자야?

D: 글쎄요. 곧 알게 되겠죠!

**lie**

D: 고장 났어요… 완전히요! … 엔진이나 … 다른 부품이 고장인 거죠!

J: 어제저녁까지는 멀쩡했잖아! 그래서 올리브를 미행해서 캠벨 저택으로 갔고.

D: 알았어요… 어떻게 된 거냐면…

J: 알고 싶지 않아! 정말이야! … 처음엔 둘이 데이트를 하더니 그러다 갑자기 관뒀지! … 그리고 넌 죽상을 하고 다녔어. 난 생각했지. "그래, 그냥 여자야. 이겨낼 거야." 며칠이 지난 지금… 넌 멍한 얼굴로 여기 앉아 있고 차는 없어졌고, 갑자기 일도 뒷전이 된 거야.

D: 그렇게 간단한 게 아니에요! 엄마, 차를 빌려줄 거예요, 말 거예요? 얼른 말해 주세요. 20분 뒤에 버스가 떠나니까요!

J: 그래, 알았다! … 그럴 만한 가치가 있는 여자야?

D: 글쎄요. 곧 알게 되겠죠!

## Communication situations  p. 30~31

**Husband:** [하품] 토요일 아침 커피? 고마워, 여보. 맛있는 커피 한 잔으로 주말을 시작하는 것은 좋지. 오늘은 뭘 할까? 무슨 계획 있어?

**Dialogue 1**

**Wife:** 집을 좀 치워야 하지 않을까?

**Husband:** 아, 그렇게 말해 줘서 다행이야. 그러면, 어떻게 할까? 집안일을 어떻게 나누지?

**Wife:** 내가 정원이랑 작업장을 맡을게.

**Husband:** 집은 나한테 맡기겠다는 뜻이야?

**Wife:** 나는 4시에 애들을 데리러 가야 해. 당신을 도울 수 없을 거야.

**Husband:** 아 이런… 나 혼자 다 하진 않을 거야. 나는 그냥 빨래만 해야겠어.

**Wife:** 그래. 식기세척기에 그릇도 넣어줄 수 있어?

**Husband:** 그럼, 물론이지. 그릇 넣고 버튼 하나 누르는 건 일도 아니야. 이따 봐.

### Dialogue 2

**Wife:** 집에서 책이나 읽으려고 해. 당신은?

**Husband:** 시내 중심부에 새로 생긴 백화점에 가고 싶어. 하지만 가는 길에 도로 공사 하는 데가 있을 것 같은데 어떻게 그곳에 어떻게 가야 할지 모르겠어.

**Wife:** 내비게이션을 사용하는 게 어때?

**Husband:** 말도 안 되는 소리 마. 내가 그 장치 싫어하는 거 알잖아. 그래서 다시 한 번 말하면, 어떻게 그곳까지 가지?

**Wife:** 다리로 가서 첫 번째 코너에서 좌회전해야 할 것 같은데.

**Husband:** 아냐, 안 돼. 첫 번째 좌회전 코너는 폐쇄되었어. 곧장 앞으로 가야겠다.

**Wife:** 그래. 그런 다음에 길을 따라 신호등까지 가.

**Husband:** 코너에 영화관이 있지?

**Wife:** 맞아. 영화관에서 좌회전해.

**Husband:** 알았어. 그 다음에는?

**Wife:** 300미터 직진하면 오른쪽에 백화점이 있어.

**Husband:** 알았어. 그럼 쉽겠네. 고마워.

### Dialogue 3

**Wife:** 나는 작업장에서 일할 거야.

**Husband:** 정확히 무슨 일을 할 건데?

**Wife:** 음, 잔디 깎는 기계를 수리할 필요가 있거든.

**Husband:** 맞아, 정원 전체를 약간 손봐야 할 것 같더라.

**Wife:** 그러게. 잔디 깎는 기계를 수리하고 나면, 낙엽도 긁어모으고 잔디도 깎을 거야.

**Husband:** 그러면 좋겠군. 물도 줄 거야?

**Wife:** 응. 대신에 집은 당신이 맡아 줄래?

**Husband:** 물론이지, 그렇게 하자.

# Scene 4 (16)

### Film dialogue and vocabulary  p. 34~36

**O:** 물건은 오늘 전해드리도록 하죠! 오늘이요! 오후 비행기로 미국에 돌아갈 거예요!

**C:** 그건 안 됩니다! 조심해야 하거든요. 당신이 올드 베리에서 일을 망친 덕분이죠. 경찰에선 움직임이 없지만, 로버트 머리가 뭔가 일을 꾸미고 있을 겁니다.

O: 무슨 일요?

C: 그에 대해 당신한테 말 안 한 게 있어요. 일단은 안전한 곳을 찾아서 숨어 있어요.

A: 그럼, 뭐가 잘못된 건지 알 수 있을까?

O: 아니, 안 돼.

O: 깨끗한 차가 필요해! 큰 건 아니더라도, 당장 필요해!

A: 문제없어. 뒤에 주차된 두 대 중에 하나 골라. 한 대에 5천이야.

O: 영국 화폐로 5천 파운드라고? 원래 훨씬 싸게 주잖아!

A: 그래, 근데 네가 곤경에 빠진 것 같으니깨! 나한테는 돈 벌 기회인 거지!

O: 이 매정한 자식! 그만한 현금은 없단 말이야!

`negotiate`

O: 현금 2천에다 밖에 주차된 차까지 줄게.

A: 색깔이 맘에 안 들어. 하지만… 좋아! 그렇게 해! 그래, 그래… 현금 2천에다 밖에 주차된 차까지 줘. (…) 좋아! 거래는 끝났으니 뭐 좀 마셔야지! 차 끓여 줄까? 아니면 커피? 먹을 것 좀 줄까?

O: 그거 좋겠네. 음식은 얼마야? 천 파운드?

`leave`

A: 그래, 그래… 현금 2천에다 밖에 주차된 차까지 줘. (…) 좋아! 거래는 끝났으니 뭐 좀 마셔야지! 차 끓여 줄까? 아님 커피? 먹을 것 좀 줄까?

O: 그거 좋겠네. 음식은 얼마야? 천 파운드?

### Communication situations  p. 40~41

**TV host:** 신사 숙녀 여러분, 다시 오신 것을 환영합니다! 여러분은 지금 '누가 더 크게 부자가 되고 싶은가'의 시즌 10을 시청하고 계십니다. 저는 커티스와 함께 있는데요, 그는 505파운드를 받을 수 있는 마지막 질문에 대답할 겁니다. 커티스, 준비됐나요?

`Dialogue 1`

**Curtis:** 그 어느 때보다도 준비되어 있습니다!

**TV host:** 좋습니다. 시작하죠. 커티스, 1킬로미터는 몇 마일일까요?

**Curtis:** 영국 법정 표준으로요, 아니면 해상으로요?

**TV host:** 오, 좋은 지적이네요! 물론 영국 법정 표준입니다. 답이 무엇이죠, 커티스?

**Curtis:** 1킬로미터는 영국 법정 표준으로 0.6214마일입니다.

**TV host:** 네, 그렇죠! 브라보. 계속할 준비가 되었나요? 1,001파운드 짜리 질문으로 시작해 봅시다. 1야드는 몇 피트인가요?

**Curtis:** 1야드는 3피트입니다.

**TV host:** 맞습니다! 브라보, 커티스! 계속할까요?

Curtis: 네, 몸풀기 중이에요.

TV host: 좋습니다! 계속 진행될수록, 게임은 점점 더 까다로워지거든요… 커티스, 1인치는 몇 센티미터죠?

Curtis: 또 수학 문제인가요? 공정하지 않잖아요!

TV host: 모든 문제는 컴퓨터에 의해 무작위로 선정된다는 점을 다시 한번 상기해 드립니다. 그러니 투정 부리지 말고 싸우십시오! 돈이 기다리고 있습니다! 그리고 사람들도 지켜보고 있어요!

### Dialogue 2

Curtis: 네, 해 보죠!

TV host: 바로 그 자세입니다! 4가지 대중교통의 이름을 대시되 알파벳 순으로 말씀해 주세요.

Curtis: 서브웨이, 트램, 튜브, 그리고 언더그라운드입니다.

TV host: 축하합니다, 알파벳은 분명 잘 아시네요! 하지만 나열하신 네 가지 중 세 개는 같은 의미입니다.

Curtis: 맞아요. 그게 잘못되었나요?

TV host: 이번 답을 인정해도 될지 잘 모르겠네요.

Curtis: 왜요?

TV host: 아, 음. 저희가 낸 질문에 해석의 여지가 너무 많았던 것 같습니다.

Curtis: 제 문제는 아니군요. 저는 정답을 말했으니까요.

TV host: 그랬죠. 인정합니다. 잠시 광고 방송 시간을 가진 후에 쇼를 계속하지요.

### Dialogue 3

TV host: 1야드는 몇 피트일까요?

Curtis: 흠, 잘 모르겠네요.

TV host: 커티스, 구명부표가 4개 있는데요. 하나 사용하시겠어요?

Curtis: 지금이 사용해야 할 때일까요?

TV host: 당신 게임이고 당신 결정입니다, 커티스. 제가 당신 대신 결정해 줄 수는 없어요.

Curtis: '사람들에게 조르기' 찬스를 써야겠어요.

# Scene 5 (17)

### Film dialogue and vocabulary   p. 44~46

C: "냇가의 세 시골 소녀." 프란체스코 마치니 작품입니다. 멋지죠?

C: 그는 주로 여체의 아름다움을 다뤘죠. 유채화이고 70×50cm. 나무 액자는 진품이 아니죠. 그래서 아주 저렴합니다. 1만5천 파운드밖에 안 해요! 실망했군요? 이해해요! 하지만 속상해할 필요 없어요! 손님이 좋아할 만한 더 저렴한 것도 있으니까! "남자의 힘"이라는 작품이죠!

D: 그런데 보기엔… 아니, 아주 큰…

**C:** 맞아요! 높이가 거의 2m나 되죠! 아주 인상적이죠! 하지만 싸구려 석고로 만든 거예요! … 말해 봐요… 원하는 게 뭐죠?

**D:** 올리브 그린요! 제가 찾아야 해요! 둘이 예전에… 같이 일한 거 아니까 어디 있는지 아시면 말해 주셔야 해요!

**C:** 두 가지만 말해 주죠, 젊은이. 첫째, 난 아무것도 해야 할 필요가 없어요. 둘째, 난 그런 이름의 사람은 몰라요.

**make a threat**

**D:** 거짓말! 당신에 대해 다 알아요! 올리브가 당신한테 그림을 훔쳐다 줬잖아요! 어디 있는지 말해 주세요! 제 동료들 데리고 다시 오길 바라는 건 아니죠?

**C:** 손님 양반, 난 아무것도 몰라요… 올리브 그린? 내가 절도범과 일했다고? 그거 재밌네! 난 정직한 미술상이라고요! 모든 작품은 완전히 합법적인 거요!

**D:** 올리브가 어디 있는지 알아야 해요!

**C:** 마르코!

**ask politely**

**D:** 올리브를 해치려는 게 아니에요! 도우려는 거예요! 제발 말씀해 주시겠어요?

**C:** 손님 양반, 난 아무것도 몰라요… 올리브 그린? 내가 절도범과 일했다고? 그거 재밌네! 난 정직한 미술상이라고요! 모든 작품은 완전히 합법적인 거요!

**D:** 올리브가 어디 있는지 알아야 해요!

**C:** 마르코!

## Communication situations  p. 50~51

**C:** 10시가 막 지났는데 벌써 손님이 오셨군요! 안녕하세요! 호기심의 방에 오신 것을 환영합니다! 무엇을 도와드릴까요, 손님?

**Dialogue 1**

**Client:** 안녕하세요. 명작을 찾고 있는데요.

**Owner:** 제대로 찾아오셨군요. 어떤 종류의 명작에 관심이 있으시죠? 그림? 조각? 장식 공예?

**Client:** 그림을 생각하고 있어요.

**Owner:** 그림은 1층에 있습니다. 그쪽으로 가시죠. 그동안, 어떤 종류의 회화에 관해 이야기할까요?

**Client:** 저는 현대 미술에 관심이 있어요.

**Owner:** 오 그러시군요. 현대 미술이 지금 아주 유행이죠. 크기는요?

**Client:** 그건 중요하지 않아요.

**Owner:** 그렇다면 어떤 것을 찾으시나요?

**Client:** 시사하는 바가 큰 그림을 원해요.

**Owner:** 좋습니다! 그렇다면 이 그림은 어떠세요? 검은색 바탕에 하얗고 약간 흐릿한 점들이 찍혀 있는, 그냥 평범한 그림처럼 보이지요. 하지만…

### Dialogue 2

**Client:** 저는 과거의 흔적들을 찾고 있어요. 그런 게 있는지 궁금하네요.

**Owner:** 손님, 주변을 한번 둘러보세요. 이곳의 모든 것이 과거에서 온 것입니다. 자, 무엇을 찾고 계시지요?

**Client:** 오르골을 생각했어요.

**Owner:** 손님께 안성맞춤인 것이 있습니다. 아주 오래되고 아름답지요. 여기를 보세요.

**Client:** 진짜 진주인가요?

**Owner:** 물론입니다! 어떤 공작부인의 소유물이었지요.

**Client:** 그럴 줄 알았어요. 태엽은 어떻게 감나요?

**Owner:** 이 자그마한 태엽 감개로요. 정말 특별한 숙녀분을 위한 고급스러운 장식품이죠.

**Client:** 확실히 예뻐 보이네요. 어떤 곡이 나오나요?

**Owner:** 작동은 이제 안 됩니다, 안타깝게도요.

**Client:** 오르골인데 음악이 나오지 않는다는 말씀이신가요?

**Owner:** 안타깝지만 그렇습니다. 하지만 진주는 진짜고 덮개에 달린 원석들도 진짜라는 점은 보증해 드릴 수 있어요.

### Dialogue 3

**Client:** 약혼녀를 위한 선물을 찾고 싶어요. 약혼녀가 골동품을 아주 좋아하거든요.

**Owner:** 숙녀분을 위한 선물이라고요! 멋지군요! 생각하고 계신 것이 있나요?

**Client:** 보석함이 좋을 것 같아요.

**Owner:** 그렇다면 멋진 장식함을 찾고 계시는군요. 어디 보자. 이건 어떠세요?

**Client:** 너무 수수해요. 전혀 감동을 주지 못할 거예요.

# Scene 6 (18)

## Film dialogue and vocabulary  p. 54~55

**D:** 올리브가 적을 만들어서 지금 놈들한테 쫓기고 있어요. 내가 먼저 찾아서 사태 해결을 도와야 한다고요.

**A:** 불쌍한 것, 당최 감을 못 잡고 있네… 정말 돕고 싶은 건지 누가 알겠어? 사실 올리브를 본 지 오래됐어! 8월에 런던에 왔었는데 만나지도 못했어. 듣기로는 여기서 무슨 과학 연구를 하고 미국으로 돌아갔다던데… 내가 아는 건 그게 다야! 내 연락처야. 며칠 뒤에 연락해! 뭔가 나올지도 모르지!

**D:** 고마워요! 많은 도움이 됐어요.

**attack Alfie**
**A:** 내가 좋아하는 거야! 과일 향이 나거든!

**don't attack Alfie**
**D:** 그냥 만나게만 해줘요! … 제발 도와줘요! (…) 안 먹어요!

A: 정말 만나고 싶다면 선택의 여지가 없을 텐데! (…) 잘했어!

## Communication situations    p. 58~59

**Radio host:** 안녕하세요, 여러분. 월요일 아침인데요, 이제 "우리 지역의 영웅"이라는 주간 방송을 시작하려고 합니다. 오늘은 제시카 오언을 모셨습니다, 올드 베리 B&B의 주인이죠. 그녀는 서비스, 음식 면에서 최고의 B&B 국제 대회 우승자입니다. 제시카는 자신이 어떻게 정상에 올랐는지, 무엇이 자신을 그렇게 강인한 사업가로 만들었는지 알려주시기로 했습니다. 어서 오세요, 제시카, 와 주셔서 고맙습니다. 먼저 본인의 배경에 관해 이야기해 보죠.

### Dialogue 1

**Jessica:** 안녕하세요, 톰, 안녕하세요, 여러분. 무슨 이야기로 시작할까요?

**Radio host:** 먼저 본인의 어린 시절과 학창시절 이야기를 해 보죠.

**Jessica:** 음, 저는 사실 올드 베리에서 태어났어요.

**Radio host:** 그렇다면 토박이시군요.

**Jessica:** 네, 맞아요. 게다가 학교 교육도 대부분 올드 베리에서 끝냈죠.

**Radio host:** 직업학교는 제외하고요, 그렇죠?

**Jessica:** 네. 직업학교는 에든버러에서 다녔어요.

**Radio host:** 왜 그렇게 고향에서 먼 곳을 선택했지요?

**Jessica:** 그렇게 오랫동안 이 마을을 떠나 있을 기회가 두 번 다시는 없을 것 같았거든요.

**Radio host:** 그 생각이 맞았나요?

**Jessica:** 처음에는 약간 고향이 그리웠지만 잘한 결정이었어요.

**Radio host:** 지금은 이 정도로 하고요, 곧 다시 이야기하죠. 채널을 고정해 주세요.

### Dialogue 2

**Radio host:** 제시카, 지금 20년 넘게 가업을 이어오고 계세요. 어떻게 이 모든 것이 시작되었나요?

**Jessica:** 중등학교 졸업 후 직업 훈련을 받으러 대학에 다녔어요.

**Radio host:** 그리고 대학은 훨씬 더 큰 도시에 있었고요.

**Jessica:** 네, 그러고는 1년간 미국에 가 있었어요.

**Radio host:** 그렇군요. 분명 훌륭한 경험이었겠네요. 유용한 지식을 갖추고 일할 준비가 모두 끝난 상태로 돌아오셨겠어요.

**Jessica:** 오 그럼요! 머리에 아이디어를 가득 담고 돌아왔죠.

**Radio host:** 그다음에는 무슨 일이 있었나요?

**Jessica:** 국제 기업에서 일을 시작했어요.

**Radio host:** 인생에서 좋았던 시기였나요?

**Jessica:** 네. 결국 저는 최고 경영진의 일원이 되었지요.

**Radio host:** 알겠습니다, 제시카, 이제 잠시 광고 시간을 갖죠. 채널을 고정해 주세요.

### Dialogue 3

**Jessica:** 네, 좋아요. 준비됐어요.
**Radio host:** 그럼, 간단히 말하죠. 중등학교를 졸업한 다음, 직업학교에서 교육을 계속 받으셨어요. 그다음에는 1년간 공백기를 가진 후에 돌아와서 기업에서 근무하셨고요. 그런데 인생이 늘 순탄하진 않았지요.
**Jessica:** 뭐랄까, 저는 항상 인생의 밝은 면을 보려고 노력해요.

# Scene 7 (19)

## Film dialogue and vocabulary   p. 62~63

**A:** 생각이 바뀌었어. 차 말고 대신 커피를 마시자고. 긴 밤이 될 테니까.
**O:** 죽이면 안 돼!
**A:** 죽일 거야! … 비스킷도 좀 있는데 안 나눠 줄 거야. 내가 아끼는 거거든! 이성적으로 생각해! 경찰이야. 골칫거리라고! 너와 나에 대해 너무 많이 알아. 게다가, 질투 나. 네가 저 멍청이한테 호감 있는 게 분명해!
**O:** 호감 없어… 아무에게도. 멍청하다고 해도 죽이면 안 돼!
**A:** 왜? 너 이 일에 너무 감정적이야! 여자들은 정에 약해서 탈이야!
**O:** 알피, 안 돼!
**A:** 내 총이잖아! 어디에서 났어?
**O:** 화장실. 사방에 총이 숨겨져 있지! 넌 강박증이야!
**D:** 뒤를 봐!
**A:** 겨우 한 놈이잖아! 우리가 처리할 수 있지, 안 그래?

**C:** 아니라네, 친구들! 아니야!

## Communication situations   p. 67

**Jessica:** 좋은 소식이야, David! 이번 달 예약이 꽉 찼구나. 이제, 아주 많은 사람을 접대할 준비를 해야 해. 음식을 비축해 놔야겠어.

### Dialogue 1

**David:** 정말 좋은 소식이네요, 엄마.
**Jessica:** 그러게! 그래서 주방에서 네 도움이 필요해.
**David:** 제가 장을 봐서 물건을 대량으로 사놓을 수 있어요.
**Jessica:** 바로 그게 네가 할 일이란다. 여기 목록이 있어.
**David:** 알았어요. 한번 볼게요.

Jessica: 내 글씨를 읽을 수 있겠니?

David: 당근 한 봉지, 콩 통조림, 그리고 시금치요.

Jessica: 맞아. 그리고 신선한 시금치가 필요해. 냉동이나 통조림은 안 돼, 명심하렴!

### Dialogue 2

David: 초밥을 시도해 보셔도 되겠네요. 요즘 인기가 아주 좋아요.

Jessica: 오 David, 초밥을 하기에는 내 나이가 너무 많아. 그리고 나는 전통 영국 요리가 더 좋단다.

David: 베이컨 에그 말씀하시는 거예요? 그리고 기름에 구운 소시지요?

Jessica: 심술부리지 말렴, David. 나는 손님 드시라고 요리하는 거야, 너 먹으라고 요리하는 게 아니라. 그런데, 내가 한 음식이 그렇게 싫으면 스스로 요리를 해 보는 게 어떠니?

# Scene 8 (20)

### Film dialogue and vocabulary  p. 70~71

O: 내가 여기 있는 건 어떻게 알았죠?

C: 마르코가 온종일 네 친구를 미행했어.

A: 내가 멍청이라고 했잖아. 대체 누구야?

O: 알피, 클로티에 씨와 인사해. 미술상이지. 몇 년 전에 동업했었어.

C: 동업? 배은망덕한 것! 그림 훔치는 기술은 다 내가 가르쳤어. 내 고객들한테도 소개해 줬고. 내가 너한테 투자한 게 얼만데!

O: 다 갚았어요! 몇 년 동안 그림을 훔쳐다 줬는데 당신은 푼돈만 줬잖아요! 내가 부자로 만들어줬잖아요.

C: 그러고는 날 배신했지! 고객들도 거의 다 가로챘고! … 그래서 널 죽이러 온 거야!

O: 잘해 봐, 이 이중인격자!

C: 알피. 알피라고 불러도 되겠나? 내 차에 가방이 있는데 그 안에 5만 파운드가 있네! 그걸 주지! 그 대신 날 도와서 올리브와 저 친구를 죽여야 하네!

O: 알피, 며칠 뒤에 내가 훨씬 더 많이 줄게…

C: 진짜 줄 수도 있고, 아닐 수도 있지. 하지만 나한텐 현금이 있어! 엄청난 현금을 당장 줄 수 있어!

O: 알피, 저 사람 말 듣지 마! 우리의 특별한 우정을 생각해 봐!

#### accept the offer
A: 미안해, 올리브. 우리 사이에 "특별한 우정" 따위 없는 거 알잖아. 총 안 버리면 친구가 죽어.

#### reject the offer
A: 거절하겠어. 남자는 죽여도 올리브는 안 돼.

C: 이해해! 하지만, 알피, 다시 생각해 봐! 올리브를 쫓고 있는 자들이… 자네가 누군지 뭘 하는지도 알아. 분명히 알아둬. 올리브는 이제 골칫거리야! 이 모든 걸… 다 잃고 싶지 않을 텐데!

A: 그 말이 맞아! 미안해, 올리브. 우리의 특별한 우정은 끝이야. 총 안 버리면 친구가 죽어!

## Communication situations  p. 76-77

**Olive:** 또 폭풍이 쳐서, 또 정전되었네요. 텔레비전도 안 나오고 인터넷도 안 되죠. 그러니, 또 "실화" 놀이를 할까요? 그랬더니 지난주에 시간이 정말 빨리 갔잖아요.

### Dialogue 1

**Jessica:** 그래요! 저는 증조할머니 이야기를 나누고 싶어요.

**Olive:** 좋아요, 저는 가족사를 좋아해요. 특히 실제로 일어났던 일이라면요.

**Jessica:** 그분은 1895년 런던 인근의 작은 마을에서 태어나셨어요.

**Olive:** 음울해질 것 같네요.

**Jessica:** 가난한 대가족이었어요. 그분은 9명 중 막내셨죠.

**Olive:** 이런! 여러 가지 의미로 자녀 수가 특이하군요.

**Jessica:** 기다려 봐요. 어느 날, 서커스단이 마을을 찾아왔어요.

**Olive:** 서커스단요? 왜! 그래서요?

**Jessica:** 서커스 단장이, 그분을 주면 큰돈을 주겠다고 가족에게 약속했죠.

**Olive:** 하지만 부모님은 동의하지 않으셨겠죠?

**Jessica:** 동의하지 않았지만, 서커스 단원들이 그분을 유괴했어요.

**Olive:** 오 안 돼요! 끔찍해요! 증조할머니가 몇 살이셨나요?

**Jessica:** 6살 정도요. 다행히 이튿날 간신히 탈출하셨어요.

**Olive:** 정말 똑똑하고 용감한 소녀였네요! 하지만 정말 무서운 이야기예요!

### Dialogue 2

**Jessica:** 사실, 어제 저에게 일어났던 일을 이야기하고 싶어요.

**Olive:** 아 그래요? 좋아요, 들어 보죠.

**Jessica:** 평소처럼 금요일 오후에, 장을 보고 있었어요…

**Olive:** … 그런데 이상한 소리를 들으셨군요…

**Jessica:** 아, 그만해요! 어떤 남자가 저를 부르는 소리가 들렸어요.

**Olive:** 신비롭고 기왕이면 잘생긴 낯선 사람이 나타나는 거죠! 계속하세요.

**Jessica:** 처음에는 무시했는데 계속 부르는 거예요.

**Olive:** 그쯤 되니 걱정되시지 않던가요? 그 남자 참 고집불통이네. 어떻게 하셨어요?

**Jessica:** 결국 멈춰 서서 이렇게 물어봤지요. 왜 저를 따라오시죠?

**Olive:** 그러니까 어떻게 반응하던가요?

**Jessica:** 그 남자가 미소를 짓더니 말했어요. "부인, 제 카트를 가져가셨어요."

**Olive:** 오 이런! 창피해라! 그래도 그분이 신사적으로 나와서 다행이네요.

# Scene 9 (21)

## Film dialogue and vocabulary    p. 80~81

**A:** 재킷 정말 고마워, 데이비드!

**A:** 요즘 잉글랜드에는 시체 묻기 좋은 데를 찾기가 쉽지 않아. 여기가 인기가 많지. 여기에 많은 무덤을 팠어! 대부분 저 무덤보다는 예쁘지! 무덤은 1.5m 이상은 파야 해. 너무 얕으면 경찰이나 주민들한테 시체가 발각돼. 야생동물이 발견되기도 하고.

**C:** 준비됐나?

**A:** 네… 그런 것 같아요.

**C:** 젠장! 못하겠어. 이런 건 잘 안 한단 말이야. 5분만 줘. 혼자 있고 싶어.

**A:** 잠깐만요! 내가 원래는 담배를 끊었지만 한 대 피워야겠어요.

**O:** 데이비드, 그만해요!

**O:** 데이비드! 지금이에요!

**D:** 기꺼이!

## Communication situations    p. 84~85

**Pollster:** 실례지만, 5분만 시간을 내주실 수 있나요? 저는 환경 보호와 관련된 프로젝트를 운영하는 비정부 기구에서 나왔습니다. 몇 가지 질문에 대답해 주시겠어요?

### Dialogue 1

**Passer-by:** 물론이죠. 저도 열렬한 환경 보호론자니까 기꺼이 질문에 답해 드릴게요.

**Pollster:** 잘됐군요. 자, 첫 번째 질문은, 우리 지구가 어떻게 보호될 수 있을까요?

**Passer-by:** 음, 할 수 있는 사소한 일이 많죠.

**Pollster:** 예를 들면요?

**Passer-by:** 절약될 수 있는 물부터 시작해 보죠.

**Pollster:** 그러면 여기서 고전적인 예는 '면도할 때 수도꼭지를 잠가라'가 되겠네요.

**Passer-by:** 아니면 '목욕 대신 샤워를 해라'도 있죠.

**Pollster:** 그렇지요, 충분히 할 수 있는 일이죠, 고생스럽긴 하겠지만요.

**Passer-by:** 아니면 빗물을 받아서 다른 용도로 재사용할 수도 있어요.

**Pollster:** 맞습니다, 추가적인 노동이 조금 필요하겠지만 물론 할 수 있는 일이죠.

**Passer-by:** 그럼, 이제 다 됐나요?

**Pollster:** 네. 시간 내주셔서 감사합니다!

### Dialogue 2

**Passer-by:** 알았어요, 하지만 몇 가지만이에요.
**Pollster:** 물론이죠, 약속드린 대로입니다. 우리 지구와 생태계 전체가 어떤 식으로 파괴되고 있는지 아시나요?
**Passer-by:** 네, 물론 알죠.
**Pollster:** 예를 들어 주실 수 있나요?
**Passer-by:** 열대 우림이 벌목됩니다.
**Pollster:** 그래서 그 결과는 어떻지요?
**Passer-by:** 야생동물이 멸종될 위기에 처했어요.
**Pollster:** 맞아요, 정말 안타깝지요..
**Passer-by:** 그럼, 이제 다 됐나요?
**Pollster:** 네, 시간 내주셔서 감사합니다!

### Dialogue 3

**Passer-by:** 하시는 일은 좋게 생각하지만 제가 지금 바빠서요. 죄송합니다.
**Pollster:** 그러시군요. 괜찮습니다. 좋은 하루 보내세요.

### Dialogue 4

**Passer-by:** 물론이죠. 저도 열렬한 환경 보호론자니까 기꺼이 질문에 답해 드릴게요.
**Pollster:** 잘됐군요. 자, 첫 번째 질문은, 우리 지구가 어떻게 보호될 수 있을까요?
**Passer-by:** 우선, 재생 가능한 자원이 고려되어야 해요.
**Pollster:** 그런가요? 계속 말씀해 주세요.
**Passer-by:** 예를 들면, 에너지가 태양에서 발생하는 태양열 발전소가 있죠.
**Pollster:** 네, 전적으로 동의합니다.
**Passer-by:** 게다가 태양열 발전소는 다른 발전소들에 비해 비교적 저렴하게 지을 수 있어요.
**Passer-by:** 그럼, 이제 다 됐나요?
**Pollster:** 네, 시간 내주셔서 감사합니다!

# Scene 10 (22)

## Film dialogue and vocabulary     p. 88~89

**A:** 처음 사람을 쏘는 건 낙하산 훈련이랑 비슷해요. 한 번만 하고 나면 아무 생각 없어지죠!
**C:** 정확히 몇 명이나 죽여 봤지?
**A:** 어려운 질문이네요! … 대부분은 군에 있을 때 죽인 사람들이에요. 그 유명한 공수특전단… 우린 최고였죠! 그때가 좋았는데!

C: 방금 들었나?

O: 알피, 총 넘겨!

### negotiate

O: 알피, 이럴 필요 없어! 총 내려놓고 런던으로 가는 거야. 클로티에가 주기로 한 돈은… 네가 가져!

A: 그거 괜찮군! 하지만 이 자식은… 이 숲에 남는 거야.

### shoot at Alfie

A: 정신 나갔어? 날 쏜 거야? 가장 친한 친구라고! (…) 데이비드, 와우! 주먹이 나만큼 센데! 하지만 이건 알아둬. 내가 너한테 못되게 군 건 맞아! 그건 올리브가 나보다 널 좋아하기 때문이야! 그냥 털어버리자고, 알았지?

D: 당연하지!

A: 정말? … 젠장!

## Communication situations    p. 92~93

**Publisher:** 이게 당신이 우리를 위해 쓸 최초의 독립적인 기사가 될 테니, 우리는 철저하게 논의해야 해요. 아시겠지만 저는 역동적이고 위험하고, 정말로 아드레날린을 분비시킬 수 있는 기사라면 좋겠어요. 자, 무엇에 관해 쓸 건가요?

### Dialogue 1

**Journalist:** 믿어 주셔서 감사합니다. 기사는 스턴트맨에 관한 것이 될 거예요.

**Publisher:** 스턴트맨이요? 정말 참신하군요. 그런데 스턴트맨의 무엇에 관해 이야기할 건가요?

**Journalist:** 스턴트맨이라는 직업과 다른 위험한 직업을 비교할 거예요.

**Publisher:** 예를 들면요?

**Journalist:** 스턴트맨이 되면 소방관이 되는 것만큼이나 부상을 많이 당하지요.

**Publisher:** 뭐라고요? 농담하는 거죠?

**Journalist:** 피부 화상을 생각해 보세요.

**Publisher:** 그렇군요… 하지만 그들의 공통점이 그것이 다인가요?

**Journalist:** 음, 근무 중에 누가 더 많은 연기를 들이마시는지도 궁금해요.

**Publisher:** 그런 대결이라면 소방관이 매번 우승할 것 같은데요. 하지만 기사로서는 충분하지 않아요.

**Journalist:** 표제로 "실신하는 소방관들"은 어때요?

**Publisher:** 뭐라고요? 소방관들의 의식 불명 말하는 건가요? 흠. 통계 자료로 뒷받침할 수 있겠어요?

**Journalist:** 네, 이미 많은 자료를 확보했어요.

**Publisher:** 흠. 알았어요, 안 될 것 없죠. 내일 초고를 준비해 오면 한번 볼게요.

### Dialogue 2

**Journalist:** 야호, 드디어! 절호의 기회가 왔군요! 저는 소방관에 관해 쓸 거예요.

**Publisher:** 소방관이요? 그런 식으로 독자의 마음을 끌겠다고요? 요즘에는 그냥 평범한 직업이잖아요.

Journalist: 뭐, 어떻게 나타내느냐에 달렸죠.

Publisher: 이제야 흥미로워지는군요. 계속해 보세요.

Journalist: 소방관이 경찰관보다 훌륭하다고 할 수도 있죠.

Publisher: 그건 도를 넘은 것 같은데요.

Journalist: 아니면 소방관이 침착함을 유지해야 한다고 할 수도 있죠, 긴급 의료원처럼요.

Publisher: 흠, 위험한 직업에 관해 이야기하기에는 좋은 방법일 수 있겠네요. 한번 해 보죠.

### Dialogue 3

Journalist: 좋습니다! 가장 위험한 직업의 순위는 어떨까요?

Publisher: 흠. 잘 모르겠어요. 흔해빠진 "탑텐" 차트가 되지 않도록 무엇을 포함할 예정이죠?

Journalist: 특공대원으로 시작할 거예요.

Publisher: 오, 훌륭한 생각이군요! 남성 특공대원에 관해 무엇을 쓸 건가요?

Journalist: 아니면 여성일 수도 있겠죠!

Publisher: 왜 이러세요! 여성 특공대원을 한 번이라도 본 적 있어요?

Journalist: 없지만, 찾아보려고요.

Publisher: 한 명도 못 찾을걸요. 여자는 남자보다 신체적으로 약하고 더 예민하잖아요. 여자는 보통 덜 공격적인 직업을 택하죠.

Journalist: 그런 건 고정관념일 뿐입니다!

Publisher: 그래요? 그러면 제가 틀렸다는 것을 입증해 보세요!

Journalist: 반드시 입증해 보이겠어요.

Publisher: 알았어요. 대화 기대할게요.

# Scene 11 (23)

### Film dialogue and vocabulary    p. 96~98

O: 좋아! 이제 꼼짝들 못하겠지?

O: 이제 음식이랑 생필품 좀 마련해줘야겠어. 굶어 죽거나 얼어 죽게 둘 순 없잖아, 안 그래? 그럼 돈은…

D: 클로티에 차에 5만 파운드가 있어요! 내가 가서…

A: 차에 돈이 없는 거죠?

C: 뭐? 요즘 장사가 잘 안 돼서 말이야! 진짜 돈을 주려고 했어! … 천 파운드 정도!

A: 천 파운드? 장난해요? … 따지고 보면, 4시간 일하고 천 파운드면 나쁘지 않지, 안 그래?

O: 그나마 있던 정도 다 떨어진다, 알피. 내 지갑 어디 뒀어?

A: 런던에 있는 내 정비소에. 저 녀석 것도 같이!

D: 침낭, 초소형, 방수, 35파운드! 안 돼!

D: 비상 담요, 모든 날씨 용, 6파운드! 좋았어! … 양동이! 1파운드 50펜스. 하나면 될까? 젠장! … 휴지! 일반형, 고급형? 일반형은 단돈 99펜스! 미안, 친구들! (…) 샌드위치가 필요한데요! 그런데… 살 형편이 안 돼서요. 그래서…

**haggle**

D: 만든 지 좀 됐더라고요. 사실 유통 기한이 오늘까지예요! 깎아 줄 수 있어요? 한 개에… 50펜스 어때요?

S: 그렇게 하세요!

**beg**

D: 제발요! 친구들한테 먹여야 해요. 먹을 걸 안 갖다 주면…

S: 샌드위치는 다 공짜로 가져가세요. 어차피 오래돼서 처분해야 해요. 네, 다 가져가세요! 그리고… 힘내세요.

## Communication situations  p. 102~103

**Shop assistant:** 안녕하세요, 무엇을 도와드릴까요?

### Dialogue 1

**Client:** 안녕하세요. 이곳이 슈퍼마켓인 것은 알지만 제가 길을 잃어서요.

**Shop assistant:** 걱정하지 마세요. 제가 통로를 안내해 드릴게요. 무엇을 찾으세요?

**Client:** 어디 보자. 간식이 목록 맨 처음에 있네요.

**Shop assistant:** 네, 간식은 항상 좋은 시작이죠. 그러면, 정확히 어디로 갈까요?

**Client:** 칩과 크래커 쪽으로 가죠.

**Shop assistant:** 참고로, 가장 긴 통로를 선택하셨네요. 칩은 왼쪽에 있고 크래커는 오른쪽에 있어요.

**Client:** 그럼 피스타치오와 아몬드 같은 것은요?

**Shop assistant:** 건강식품이군요. 그것들은 저쪽에 있어요. 봉지에 담아서 직접 무게를 다셔야 해요.

**Client:** 알았어요. 문제 될 거 없죠. 가서 좀 가지고 와야겠네요. 도와주셔서 감사합니다.

**Shop assistant:** 천만에요. 좋은 하루 보내세요!

### Dialogue 2

**Client:** 유제품 좀 사려고요. 여기서 살 수 있나요?

**Shop assistant:** 죄송하지만, 이곳은 편의점이에요. 기본적인 제품만 있죠. 그리고 사실 유제품은 전혀 없답니다.

**Client:** 그렇군요. 그럼 콜라 하나 살게요.

**Shop assistant:** 병에 든 것이요, 아니면 캔에 든 것이요?

**Client:** 병에 든 거요. 그리고 시원하면 좋겠어요.

**Shop assistant:** 알겠습니다. 더 필요한 것 있으세요?

**Client:** 담배 한 갑 주세요.

**Shop assistant:** 죄송하지만 손님은 18세 미만입니다. 담배를 사실 수 없어요.

### Dialogue 3

**Client:** 아직 영업 중인가요?

**Shop assistant:** 네, 그렇습니다. 무엇을 드릴까요?

**Client:** 아, 여기 쇼핑 리스트 전체가 있어요. 유제품부터 시작하죠.

**Shop assistant:** 그러세요.

**Client:** 달걀 다섯 개, 치즈 한 팩, 그리고 코티지 치즈 두 통 주세요.

**Shop assistant:** 여기 있습니다. 더 필요한 것 있으세요?

**Client:** 네. 롤빵 두 개, 도넛 두 개, 그리고 크루아상 하나 주세요.

**Shop assistant:** 그게 전부인가요?

**Client:** 그리고 콘플레이크 한 상자요. 그게 다예요.

**Shop assistant:** 여기 있습니다. 15파운드 65펜스 되겠습니다.

# Scene 12 (24)

### Film dialogue and vocabulary    p. 106~107

**D:** 20파운드나 있었으면서 어떻게 한마디도 안 할 수가 있어요!

**D:** 불쌍한 사람들! … 오래된 샌드위치를 두고 왔다고요!

**O:** 내 돈이 아니에요! 마르코 주머니에서 나왔는데 당신이 나 때문에 고생한 걸 생각하니까 밥이라도 제대로 먹여야겠더라고요.

**D:** 그래도 그 서류는 머리한테 돌려줘야 해요… 지금 벼르고 있어요! … 당신이 막을 수 있다고요! 머리는 술집에서 본 빌과는 달라요. 빌은 귀찮게 굴면 팰 수 있죠. 머리는 당신에 대한 정보도 많고 당신 인생을 악몽으로 만들 능력도 있어요. 그러니까 제발, 그만 끝내요!

**O:** 이 일을 하다 보면 권력자에게 목숨을 위협당하기 마련이에요. 부자들 그림을 훔치면 그렇게 되죠. 끝낼 수 없어요! 아직은 안 돼요! 당신은 그만둬요, 오언 순경님! 올드 베리로 돌아가서 살던 대로 살아요!

**D:** 살던 대로요? 당신이 다 망쳐놔서 돌아갈 데가 없어요. 당신한테서 못 떨어진다고요.

**O:** 그래서 난 좋은데요!

#### answer the phone

**D:** 지금은 통화 못 해요. 올리브한테 접근 중이에요!

**M:** 게나디? … 그 경찰 놈이 여자를 찾았어! 부하들을 보내서 둘 다 죽여!

**G:** 그러지!

#### ignore the call

**M:** 게나디? … 녀석이 내 전화를 안 받는데 둘이 같이 있는 것 같아! 부하들을 보내서 둘 다 죽여!

**G:** 그러지!

## Communication situations  p. 110~111

**Grandpa:** 얘야, 와 줄 수 있어서 다행이다. 이게 생긴 지 일주일이나 됐는데 어디부터 시작해야 할지 모르겠구나. 어떻게 쓰는 거니?

### Dialogue 1

**Grandchild:** 안녕하세요, 할아버지! 어떤 것을 갖고 계시는지 좀 보여 주세요.

**Grandpa:** 이 멋지고 반짝거리는 검은색 노트북이란다!

**Grandchild:** 좋아 보이네요. 어떤 운영 체제인지 한번 보죠.

**Grandpa:** 어떠니…?

**Grandchild:** 제가 아는 운영 체제네요, 그러니 문제없어요. 그런데 무슨 일로 필요하신 거예요?

**Grandpa:** 글쓰기용으로 컴퓨터가 필요하단다. 우리 가족의 역사를 써 보고 싶어.

**Grandchild:** 정말 멋진 생각이네요!

**Grandpa:** 그렇지, 나도 그렇게 생각해.

**Grandchild:** 좋아요. 이 아이콘을 클릭하고 툴바를 보세요.

**Grandpa:** 툴바가 뭐니? 아, 알았다. 이 기호는 어떤 용도지?

**Grandchild:** 눌러 보시는 게 어때요? 그게 배우는 데 가장 좋은 방법이잖아요.

**Grandpa:** 내가 뭔가 엉망으로 만들 수도 있으니까 같이 있어 주겠니?

**Grandchild:** 괜찮을 거예요! 저장하려면 디스크 아이콘을 클릭해야 한다는 것만 기억하세요.

**Grandpa:** 아 그래, 좋은 생각이구나! 고맙다, 얘야.

### Dialogue 2

**Grandchild:** 안녕하세요, 할아버지. 걱정하지 마세요. 제가 가르쳐 드릴게요. 뭔데요?

**Grandpa:** 역시 너한테 의지하면 될 줄 알았어! 자, 새로 산 스마트폰이란다. 안타깝게도, 완전히 암흑이야.

**Grandchild:** 켜셔야 해요. 여기 버튼이 있어요.

**Grandpa:** 허, 작동되는구나! 그러면, 전화 걸 준비가 된 거니?

**Grandchild:** 먼저 PIN을 입력하셔야 해요.

**Grandpa:** 그게 뭔데?

**Grandchild:** 폰의 잠금 상태를 해제할 수 있는 연속적인 숫자예요.

**Grandpa:** 아 그래, 매장에서 이야기하더라. 여기 있다. 이제 전화할 수 있는 거니?

**Grandchild:** 음, 직접 해 보시는 게 어때요?

**Grandpa:** 좋아! 너희 할머니에게 전화해야겠구나. 아주 깜짝 놀랄 거다!

### Dialogue 3

**Grandpa:** 어떻게 생각하니?

**Grandchild:** 아, 정말 좋은 기기네요, 할아버지.

**Grandpa:** 그래? 어떻게 아니?

**Grandchild:** 아주 빠른 하드 드라이브와 멀티 코어 프로세서가 있다는 것을 알 수 있어요.

**Grandpa:** 나는 하나도 못 알아듣겠지만, 네가 하는 말이니 맞겠지, 얘야.